PRAISE FOR **WHEN THE ALPHABET COMES**

"A basketball was Jerome Allen's passport from poverty to privilege and access. Privilege and access would be his undoing, almost costing him everything. This book is Allen's meditation, bringing awareness to an internal conflict; his disdain for those who possess privilege and his own unrelenting hunger for it. He takes us on a journey through a self-created storm . . . an exposure that would serve as a portal to a restored sense of self, a reexamination of his relationship with God, and a re-commitment to family and community. If you want to understand what happens after a revered sports figure falls from grace, I recommend reading When The Alphabet Comes."

—Stephanie A. Tryce, J.D. St. Joseph's University

"Jerome's memoir is timely and true to his North Philly roots. It makes you think about the 'two cultural worlds' he and many of us are forced to navigate daily. When The Alphabet Comes is a deep dive into how opportunity, wanting to fit in and our decision-making can change our lives in an instant; and a reminder that personal accountability is our path to redemption."

—Dawn Staley Head Women's Basketball Coach
University of South Carolina

"When The Alphabet Comes dangles a mirror in front of the reader, daring us to reckon with a reflection of our truest selves—what if you thought you threw it all away? Jerome's story is impossible to believe, yet he reveals himself with a degree of vulnerability that inspires us to live more courageously. Read this book to be touched by a journey through worlds that weren't supposed to intersect, to a place where family and faith are the ultimate destination."

—Michael Lintulahti Associate Athletic Director
Germantown Friends School

"An authentic testimony of truth. Whether you are an athlete, entrepreneur, CEO or work a 9-5, this powerful book teaches the importance of access and exposure and how those experiences can shape our lives."

—Chris Clark Assistant Men's Basketball Coach
Temple University

"When The Alphabet Comes is RIVITING and RAW! It was hard to put down….This is a great story of redemption that continues into his everyday life .After reading this book, you cannot help but root for Pooh and others out there like him…."

—Jada Pierce Head Women's Basketball Coach
Niagara University

"Jerome Allen's book provides basic insights about life from the vantages of a father, husband and coach. His trials, tribulations, and triumphs reflect what it means to be imperfect. It is inspiring, relatable, and authentic. It's a must-read."

—John Hampton Asst. Women's Basketball Coach
St. Joseph's University

"When The Alphabet Comes is a rare find. Jerome Allen tells a story that you think you know but don't. Allen was the first domino to fall in the "varsity blues" case that profiled the corruption of movie and television stars who were willing to do whatever to get their children in America's most prestigious universities. The writing is purposeful, colorful, and deeply reflexive. It is Norf Philly, direct and incisive, cutting through simple right and wrong. The questions Allen asks himself throughout stay with the reader – and one can't help but ask themselves what would I do? You get to know him, worry for him. But he wants no pity. And, in true hip hop fashion, Allen is honest, vulnerable, strong, humble, guilty and innocent – quintessentially human.

— Dr. Scott N. Brooks Associate Professor of Sociology Director (Int.) Sanford School of Social and Family Dynamics

WHEN
THE ALPHABET
COMES

a life changed by exposure

JEROME ALLEN

AIDA

11,563,200 minutes equals 192,720 hours.

And 192,720 hours equals 8,030 days

And 8,030 days equals 1,147 weeks.

And 1,147 weeks equals 264 months.

And 264 months equals 22 years.

That's how long you have been on your knees

fiercely praying for my covering.

Your efforts haven't gone unnoticed.

Your significance has pushed me forward.

I don't know where I'd be without you.

I love you and I thank you for being

the prayer warrior that you are.

CONTENTS

FOREWORD

On July 11, 2019, I flew to Vegas to take my physical for the Washington Wizards. Right before I got on the plane, Jamal Crawford called and asked me when was the last time I talked to Jerome. He said Sports Illustrated has just released an article, and that I should call and check on him. He sent the link, I read the article, then I picked up the phone.

Jerome answered. And I responded with three questions, all at once—"Fam, what's good? You alright? Where you at?" I could hear the smile on his face as he was saying, I'm in Vegas, baking." Normally, I would have thought he was referring to the outside temperature of a typical NBA Summer League Day. But this time, I actually thought he was reacting to the SI article, so I said, "For real?"

When The Alphabet Comes: A Life Changed by Exposure, is simply that. Jerome went through it and penned it. I read it and received it. His life was changed by exposure. And so was mine. For two NBA seasons, Jerome and I worked together. During that time, I experienced the happiest day of my life and the saddest—I married the love of my life and I buried my little sister. Jerome flew to Seattle to attend both.

I remember taking the charter flight back to Boston after the funeral, when the plane didn't land until 6 a.m. and we had a game against the Wizards at 1 p.m. I went home and slept for an hour. Then I got up, drove to the arena and proceeded to drop 33 on them. I was running on fumes. I was emotionally drained. But after the game, before I could sit down in the locker room, Jerome had me cornered in the hallway. He opened his note pad and started blurting out all the things I missed during the game.

We won the game, I scored 33 points and didn't get any sleep the night before. But Jerome didn't care, he still had a sheet full of bullet points. On this possession you didn't trust your teammate enough to make the extra pass. On another possession, you settled versus the switch. You took too many contested pull-ups. You didn't encourage your teammate after he made a mistake. You was careless with the ball late in the game. And you stopped directing the ball on D in the 4th. I mean, there had to be at least eight things on his list.

When I read When The Alphabet Comes, I felt like Jerome was breaking down his own performance. The lessons about character, decision-making, family and faith all spilled onto his own notepad. I never knew his entire story, but after reading this book, I'm thankful for his honesty. This book will make anyone take a hard look at their own decisions.

And although Jerome couldn't guard me in his prime, I'm proud to say I still consider him a Real One!

Yours truly,

I.T.

Tacoma, What up?

#Slowgrind

PREFACE

Exposure is rarely a neutral term. It covers a vast spectrum of elements. You can be exposed to another language, to opera, violence, black-tie galas, the streets of Rome, poverty, higher education, drug use, and hip-hop. With each exposure, you'll register a reaction. You'll appreciate or denigrate what's been introduced. You'll avoid it or seek it out. But being exposed almost always suggests that someone or something is being revealed that was intentionally hidden. Whether it was hidden from the public or family or even yourself, that kind of exposure carries a negative charge. This book explores the role of exposure in my life—to the lifestyles and cultures of a world outside of the North Philadelphia neighborhood where I grew up, as well as the exposure of my actions that resulted in a federal conviction.

PROLOGUE

The alarm clock on my iPhone went off at 4 a.m. Startled by the sound, I jumped up in mid-snore. The reverberation of the needed reminder carried anxiety from sleep into this moment. My post slumber mandate never allowed my brain to reach its final cycle of REM sleep. As still as my body was in posture, there was something prohibiting me from being completely at rest. When you close your eyes, dormancy continuously repeats two phases throughout the night. Non-REM, or the non-rapid eye movement phase of sleep, allows you to fall into that good, deep sleep—the kind of sleep that replenishes the soul and energizes all cognitive functions. The REM, or the rapid eye movement phase of sleep, delivers the same brain activity and same heart rate of a person who's awake. It's the most active, and most important phase of the sleep cycle. When experienced correctly, it allows a human being to collectively and progressively be re-introduced to consciousness. When its phase is interrupted by someone or something, it forces the individual to wake up with his or her mouth open and a confused look on their face.

All of my adulthood, I've had a fear of oversleeping. I think it's from the trauma associated with my college coach's punctuality threats. "If you're early, then you're on time. If you're on time, then you're late. And if you're late, then I'll see you on the track at 5 a.m." And I hated running on the track. Even now, at times, I can wake up from a catnap and instantly begin worrying about being late for practice. I'm not even in college anymore. But thinking of those 5 a.m. runs on Franklin Field through dark winter mornings still makes my body flinch today.

I have such a fear of oversleeping, that if I have something important to do in the morning, I'll either fall asleep in an uncomfortable place, or I'll set multiple alarms. Sometimes, I'll even ask my wife to set her alarm as well. And to my request she'll always say, "For what? Isn't one alarm enough? Or you just love waking up the entire house at the crack of dawn?"

This particular morning, when my alarm went off, 1,500 miles separated me and my life partner. There have been occasions when, even in distance, I'd ask Aida to call or text to make sure I'm awake. But not this morning. Before I rested for the evening, I picked up the phone inside my hotel room and politely asked the receptionist at the Fontainebleau Hotel for a 4:05 a.m. wake up call.

There's something about white bed sheets and white comforters—the smell, the fluff, the flow that engulfs the mattress—that is so relaxing. White pillowcases accent the simplicity to make the bedding look extremely sophisticated. It's almost like these coverings can bring any space into modernism. My room inside the Fontainebleau Miami Beach Hotel resembled just that—simple, elegant, open, and plain.

By the time my second alarm sounded, I was already sitting up, feet placed on the floor. I bent over, and with both elbows placed above my kneecaps, I began to hand brush from the crown of my head to a meeting point beneath my chin. I glanced over to the neatly folded clothes that my body would soon occupy. Each article of wear rested on a chair the hotel perfectly positioned some 15 feet away from the bed. My White Cement Jordan 3 Retros were tucked underneath the chair. And the last piece of my attire rested on the floor, touching the bottom of the bed frame where it had laid all night: my backpack.

A car was arriving at 4:30 a.m. to transport me to Miami International Airport. I had roughly 20 minutes to shower, brush my teeth, get dressed, hop in the elevator, stroll across the lobby, and meet the driver at the valet stand. I love taking long showers and the better the water pressure, the longer I stay in there. But I knew this cleansing experience had to be brief. So I rushed through all the formalities, threw my clothes on, made up my bed, clutched my backpack, opened the door, turned back around to stare out the window at the dark Atlantic Ocean, then proceeded to the elevator.

Alone in the elevator, I adjusted the straps on my backpack. I don't know why I do it, but grabbing the straps always represents a moment of security. The elevator reached the lobby level and its reflective doors smoothly glided apart. When I peeked through the expanding lens of the opening doors, I couldn't believe my eyes. Eleven hundred people had just been released from a nightclub experience that seemed to be continuing throughout the lobby of the Fontainebleau Hotel. Unbeknownst to me, the hotel housed one of the most popular nightclubs in the world. I just so happened to be upstairs asleep while LIV Nightclub was delivering a captivating Sunday night escapade.

Meek Mill exposed me to the audio representation of this scene on his hit single, "Amen." But like so many who consume hip-hop, I was reciting the hook of the song because it was catchy – and not because I knew exactly what he was talking about. If it were several years ago, as we say in Philly, I would have "played the let-out." But since I was 41-years-old and long past my clubbing days, I maneuvered through the lobby like a coach demonstrating a dribbling drill. In those exercises the ball is always the precious item you're trying to protect. But this makeshift lobby obstacle course forced me to slip past nightclub defenders because I was trying to protect the $10,000 in cash I had in my backpack.

PART I

I won't complain.
REV. PAUL JONES

CHAPTER 1

WHY?

My father's voice invades my sleep again.

"Romey, wake up. Romey, do you hear me? Come on, let's go! Time to get up!

"Get up now. We got thirty minutes before the bus comes. Get dressed and feed yourself. I gotta get your sister ready."

I'm just a kid, but this might be the morning I can talk him out of going to church. I can ask him Why do we have to do this every Sunday? Why can't I stay home and play in the street with my friends or shoot on the basketball goal hanging from the pole on the corner? Down the hall, I can hear him chanting those happy, rhythmic phrases he uses on Sunday mornings. I'm planting seeds, I'm planting seeds, I may not witness the harvest, but I'm planting seeds.

Just as I'm about to call out Why to plead my case one more time, I wake up. I open my eyes and realize I'm not on the 2700 block of North Bonsall Street in Philadelphia and I am not an 8-year-old boy. I am 45 and living in a townhouse in Waltham, Massachusetts. Aida lies asleep next to me. And although we populate the same space, tons of distance lie between us.

Why had I been reminded of my dad's spiritual gardening skills while I slept? Sleep had become a precious getaway, a much-needed vacation from my waking life. And that portion of my history wasn't invited on the trip. But 39 years later, the foundation established by those compulsory Sunday morning outings had become the source that allowed God to extend forgiveness, deliver redemption, and exercise His glory in my life.

There's a spirit behind the word Why. If the question starts with why, true intent can be disguised. Presuming it's crafted properly, you can blur complaining with a request for knowledge. When events transpire and you are forced to receive the gift of suffering, do you converse with God asking why these things are happening because you sincerely want to learn, or because you're complaining?

"Lord, why are these things happening to me? I'm a good dude. I'm a good father. I've shared all the blessings you've bestowed upon me. I didn't forget, Lord. Every good thing you exposed me to, I've done the same for others. I've paid it forward. Remember the reading and math enrichment program that was held in the basement of my wife's hair salon? Well that mirrored the tutoring program that me, Cre, Smoke, and Man Man used to walk to when we were younger. You remember, Lord—the Neighborhood Activities House Association, NAHA? The resource center around the corner from Grandma's house? The place we went to get free breakfast and snacks? Remember the partnership NAHA had with students from Bryn Mawr College and Haverford College? I never forgot, Lord. I paid Philadelphia public school teachers to come in during their summer vacation to proctor age and grade-appropriate reading and math enrichment classes.

"I've served the community. I've funded STEM programs, code academies, financial literacy camps and entrepreneur workshops. Lord, I even begged the Mayor's Action Center to allow young men from our HOOD Enriched program to volunteer in their office. They answered phones, they dealt with the public. They wore button-up shirts and khaki pants. We exposed them to proper workplace etiquette, in voice and posture. The City didn't have the money in their budget to pay the kids, so I paid them a weekly salary out of my own pocket. That project was important to me, because I remembered the summer job I had working for the Department of Recreation as a teenager. I remembered Tennis Young going out of his way to give Andre and me summer jobs. Lord, I even took 55 of the HOOD Enriched kids on a coach bus to visit Clark Atlanta University and Morehouse College. That thirteen-hour bus ride was nerve-wracking. But I remember visiting Haverford College for NAHA's post tutoring program barbecue. That was my first time outside of the city, Lord. It opened my eyes. The clean streets, the trees, the big houses we saw while gazing out the windows of the yellow bus—it was so refreshing. Television didn't do the suburban landscape any justice. It looked 10 times better in person.

"I never forgot, Lord—I never forgot about youth from distressed neighborhoods. Lord, remember the trips to Italy? You allowed the game of basketball to take me all over the world. And in turn, I took city kids across the Atlantic Ocean. They visited the Roman Coliseum, and Vatican Square, even ate gelato outside of Sistine Chapel. Those kids would probably never get a chance to leave the state of Pennsylvania, let alone the country. But I made sure I added to their cultural capital.

"You kept blessing me with professional basketball contracts, and I kept blessing others. I shouldn't have to be subjected to these harsh consequences, Lord. All these works—remember how I took UPenn's basketball team to homeless shelters every Thanksgiving? I made sure all the players reflected on what it truly means to be thankful. We always started our Thanksgiving Day by serving those who were less fortunate. Afterwards, players and staff situated themselves at my home in Elkins Park so that they could devour the feast that Aida prepared. Every Thanksgiving. Lord, I made sure our players were active on campus. I challenged them to exhaust themselves in all that campus had to offer. I supported our students and student athletes alike. I went to Greek fraternity and sorority step shows. I attended Black Men United meetings on campus. I went to football games, gymnastic meets, and soccer matches. I allowed my own children to travel on the team bus, just so that I could model fatherhood. I wanted the players to see me in a role outside of being their college basketball coach. I encouraged and helped our players obtain summer internships. My college coach did it for me, and I pledged to do the same.

"Lord, I've coached, I've mentored—I've put people first. I don't understand why I am going through a season of exposure, a season of despair, a season of suffering. Why Lord? I do understand that suffering produces perseverance, and perseverance produces character. But, Lord, I already got character. There's no hope in this suffering, there's no gift. It will deliver only shame. Come on, Lord. I've prayed at night. I've given You the glory in front of an audience. I've introduced others to you. I've spoken of your goodness. I've paid my tithes. I've done— for the most part—what has been asked of me. But I don't want this gift, Lord. At the age of six, when my father first introduced me to you, I was told that you would remain faithful. Well this reveal doesn't feel like a faithful act. Plus, I can't believe you'd promote others and allow them to receive worldly fame. I haven't done any of the bullshit I've seen them do. I'm your boy, Lord. I'm not perfect, but you know I have a good heart. Why would you let them go untouched, but yet chastise me? Why Lord?"

Talking about God and talking to God can be two different things. All this chatter happened when I was in a space where it was just me and God. No audience, no companions—just me, God, and the loneliness of complaining. In an attempt at transparency, I can now admit that I wasn't asking why because I had a deep desire to understand what God was attempting to execute. I was asking why because I was complaining. I wasn't seeking knowledge. I simply wanted to bypass a season of tribulation. So, in doing so, I started tallying up all my good deeds—while bringing to God's attention either the "not so good deeds" of others, or the reciprocation of his bless-full efforts. I completely ignored two facts: first, this faith-based relationship was between Him and I. And secondly, and more importantly, I wasn't ready to admit that this was a self-created storm.

There was something else though—the biggest element dressing my ignorance was that trials and tribulations come to the just and the unjust. I walked around as if the avoidance of suffering in my life could have a correlation with the number of good deeds I performed. Almost as if I could escape trials, exposure and suffering if I'm a good person. That's the level of arrogance and pride I was displaying when I led with a complaining Why. Never mind the nutrients gained from suffering or exposure—suicide was not far from thought. I'll get even with God, because there's no way I should have to deal with this. Not me. I'd rather be dead.

In an instant, I'd forgotten my own evidence, my own story. I'd allowed arrogance and pride to blind me to of all of God's goodness. I'd allowed my will to supersede His. I'd completely ignored the affirmation behind God's refusal to let me go untouched. And therefore, it was easy to lose faith. His chastisement wasn't greeted with thankfulness. It wasn't met with the excitement that correction offers. I wasn't upset at my behavior. I was upset that I got caught.

Some of what we go through in life has nothing to do with our sins or mistakes. And some of what we go through cannot be avoided because of our righteousness. I kept saying, Lord, I'm your boy. I shouldn't have to go through this. But could it be that because I was His boy, He knew He could trust me to go through a season of exposure so that He could get the glory?

Maybe I was chosen to go through experiences, circumstances, conditions, and encounters so that something other than my comfort would be promoted. Maybe His chastisement was His way of peeling back the layers blocking my true inner man. Wait a minute. It doesn't make sense. Again, all of this happened because I had a failure in character. I'm aware that a failure in character is different from a lack of character. And God knows I don't lack character. I just passively deviated from that which I possessed. God had nothing to do with it.

So I shouldn't bring Him in it now—when I'm trying to make sense out of my own nonsense. I did say, "Lord, if you knew I couldn't handle what I prayed for, why did you give it to me?" trying to make my unpreparedness the issue. But at this point, shuffling the blame, or acknowledging that it was a self-created storm, wasn't the issue. That my integrity had not matched my platform wasn't the issue, either. The issue now was whether or not I was going to allow my ordeal to play out, while holding onto the possibility that God could get some glory out of this exposure.

CHAPTER 2

JULY 1, 2019

It's 5:30 p.m. at one of the most popular hotels in all of South Beach. The July heat index for Miami can be quite challenging. But at this time of day, the sun's slow descent, coupled with a slight ocean breeze, allows any poolside haven in southern Florida to be a glimpse of paradise. Aida allowed me to taste her drink, a combination of frozen pìna colada and strawberry daiquiri—better known as a Miami Vice. It's topped off with a white liquor of your choosing. If left up to the bartender, a "middle shelf" rum wets the crystalized flavored slush. Aida's drink was so good that I ordered one for myself. Two alcoholic drinks in a ten-minute span, that's not me at all. I've become more seasoned in life. That's just a fancy way of saying I'm old now, and the older I've gotten the more I've reduced my intake of alcohol. I don't have the desire to "get twisted" as we used to say. The reality of it though is that it takes two days for me to recover—and I don't have two days to spare. I got too much `stuff" going on. However, on this day, a drink, some atmosphere, and some stillness, is exactly what Aida and I needed.

After the drinks have been assaulted by our first sips, we both lean back in our chairs, take deep breaths, close our eyes, and simultaneously let out long ahhhhhhhhhhhhhhhhhhhhs. After carrying a huge burden of uncertainty for almost two and a half years, this day marks the removal of the boulder that's been weighting us down. For two and a half years, we've walked with an additional gravitational pull that seemed to increase with every step we took. Every forward motion increased the pressure applied to every muscle, every joint in our bodies.

Stress will make your entire body ache—literally, from head to toe. And boy, were we carrying stress. But on this day, July 1, the stress of uncertainty is being released into the atmosphere. You see, two hours prior in federal court, I received sentencing of six months of home detainment, four years of supervision, and 600 hours of community service. Months earlier, I had pled guilty to wire fraud, only to eventually return to stand before the Judge on this day to face rightful punishment. I'm not handsome to begin with, but can you imagine how my face looked: all stressed out and worried, with the fate of my life in someone else's hands? Long face, puffy eyebrows, and 46 years of accumulated wrinkles—eyes sunk in, eyeballs coated with a gloss of moisture—looking sad, old, nervous, and scared. As Jay-Z so eloquently said, "The stress'll take a young nigga, give him a old face."

Sentencing—I don't wish it on my worst enemy. This type of uncertainty will get the best of anyone. I don't care how accepting of the possibility of custodial time you are, no one, at their core, wants someone else deciding their fate. Up until the last 90 seconds, everyone inside the courtroom thought I was gonna receive the maximum of the sentencing guidelines —- 27 months of custodial time. My wife, my oldest son, my sister, my best friend, and my favorite Penn parent all sat in the courtroom ready to share the raw emotions equated with undesirable outcomes. I sat on the edge of my chair, head lowered, eyes alternating between the floor and the Judge. Every blink had a different focal point. The Judge would be just in any decision she rendered. I was just praying for the mercy of the court.

The fluctuation of emotions, the traumatic shock to the human body, gives way to the release of the long ahhhhhhhhhhh. Having a sentencing date lingering over your head for several years is tough. I prayed for God's will to be done. Quietly however, I walked in my flesh, hoping our outcomes lined up. When you're guilty of said charges, though, sometimes you don't think you deserve to receive a favorable outcome. So, as much as I believed that everything, every decision, would ultimately be for my good, I was really hoping to avoid custodial time. My exhale was a direct derivative of the case's finality. So was Aida's. However, her ahhhhhhhhh also had an undisclosed layer of neglect that covered the same time span as my case. Her happiness with the sentencing outcome was twofold. For one, I would be allowed to return to the daily activities of the life we shared. And, two, there was a possibility she could get her husband back.

I was present, but I lacked presence. For two and a half years, in every setting, in every relationship outside of our union, I remained intact. I performed fatherly duties, I drove the kids to school, and I conversed with them. I supported them at school and sporting events. I perfected masking the right sense of normalcy in their world. At work, I smiled, I coached, I assisted, and I supported. I operated as if there wasn't an elephant in the room. All was well. I was present. But my presence was not felt by my first priority. I never checked in with her, never sat next to her just to talk. I never stopped to ask how she was doing with the exposure, with the embarrassment. I never hugged her. I never assured her that all would be OK.

I wanted her to be my place of rest. And got angry when it didn't happen. But I never stopped to ask myself, where was her place of rest? No affirming dialogue, no nothing. Just compressed anger because I was being emotionally selfish. After 21 years of marriage, she deserved what I was depriving her of, especially at a time like this—when the natural balance of her nurturing spirit was being threatened by decisions she had nothing to do with. In her eyes, I was present, but I lacked presence. On July 1, 2019, she was hoping her long exhale marked the day she got her husband back. Both of our stress modules would end exactly where it all began—inside the Fontainebleau Hotel, pool side.

It was the same location, but everything had changed. I was still a husband, a father, and a basketball coach. But I was no longer here as the John R. Rockwell Head Coach of Men's Basketball at the University of Pennsylvania. And I now carried the label of a convicted felon.

CHAPTER 3

IDOLS

In the 73-year history of the National Basketball Association there have been only 25 players to play in this league who stood 5-foot-9 or shorter. Only three out of the 25 have career scoring averages above 10.0 points per game. One may argue for a fourth, who averaged 9.9 points per game. I mean, damn, he was only 5-foot-7—we can slide him one tenth of a point. And only three times has anyone from this group been selected to an All-Star Game. Today, the average height of an NBA player is 6-foot-7; conversely, the average height of an American male is 5-foot-9. So it's safe to say, average-size Americans don't play in the NBA. They just don't. You have a better chance at winning the Powerball.

Calvin Murphy is the only player in the history of the NBA to be inducted into the Naismith Basketball Hall of Fame and not be taller than 5-foot-9. In 1002 games he averaged 17.9 pts. And in 1979 he was selected to represent the Eastern Conference in the NBA All-Star Game. This would be his only appearance in such a game. On that night, in Pontiac, Michigan, the East would be led in scoring by the Philadelphia 76ers' own Julius "Dr. J" Erving.

Doc was my favorite player—and he was my idol. Not because of the afro, though. But rather because he just carried himself like a true professional. And he would dunk on you if you got in his way.

In 1979, I was too young to know anything about style and grace. But somehow, I knew Dr. J had it. The entire city of Philadelphia loved him. The entire NBA loved him. He introduced me to Coca Cola soda and Converse basketball shoes. I really thought by drinking caffeine, and letting long tube socks stand above your Converse, you'd be able to mimic his grace and flare. Regardless of how much sweat he dispensed, the afro stayed intact. He was smooth. He was my favorite. He was the Doctor.

I still remember the reverse layup from behind the backboard in the 1980 Finals. I even remember his dunk over Michael Cooper in 1983. That same year, the Sixers went on to win the NBA title. And everyone in the city was talking about the upcoming parade. I got so excited because I was finally going to see Dr. J in person. I was going to the parade. No school for me that day. Thursday, June 2, 1983, would be the day I finally met my idol. I mapped out my route: "I'm going to take the 23 trolley, then the Broad Street subway." I was ready. When I woke up that morning, I was informed by my mother that I couldn't go.

"Why?" I was too young to travel by myself and she couldn't take me because she had to go to work. "But Mom, it's the parade. Everyone from my class is going, plus Dr. J is going to be there."

"No! Now take your ass to school."

To this day I still get a little upset with her every time the word parade is mentioned. I kept saying, "Why, why mom, why can't I go?"

And she kept replying, "Cuz I said so." I kept jabbing, "That's not telling me, though."

We went back and forth for about 10 minutes straight. I wouldn't stop until she uttered, "Ask me one more time and I'm gonna whip your ass." That shut me right up. I would soon find out, some 15 years later that cuz I said so is a rule of law in parenting that demands compliance and governs a multitude of reasoning. Children want to, or rather, need to know the reasoning behind every denial. My mom knew how dangerous it was for a 10-year-old to travel to South Philadelphia by himself. I couldn't wrap my mind around it at the time. But she knew better. Currently, my youngest son is 10 years old. I'm just getting comfortable with letting him cross an intersection by himself. There's no way in the world I'd let him wander the streets of Philadelphia amongst 1.7 million fans in 1983.

Dr. J retired after the conclusion of the 1986-87 season. By that time, I had already fallen in love with the game. I became a true fan of the league. Obviously, my loyalty resided with the Sixers, but I had developed a wandering eye. With Dr. J's retirement, I needed another icon to follow. The League's popularity was growing, and coverage was expanding. By the start of the '87-88 season, I was in full mimicking mode. I was a high school freshman trying to navigate my way through a new space. Confused by the abundance of access, I defaulted to commonality.

Mo Cheeks was one of the faces of the Sixers franchise, so naturally I thought that was the style of play I had to emulate to make the varsity basketball team. As much as I respected Mo's steadiness, the insides of me were screaming for something different. So, I watched, and watched, and watched the game at both the collegiate and professional level, hoping to find someone to copy.

LaSalle College had Doug Overton and Randy Woods. Temple University had Nate Blackwell and Howie Evans. Drexel had Michael Anderson. UVA had Dawn Staley. UCLA had Pooh Richardson, and the Sixers had Mo Cheeks. I wanted to possess the same reputation that all the Philly Guards had—tough and smart; nothing fancy, just hard-nosed. I would have thrown my mother into that same descriptive category if she were an athlete. But since she didn't let me go to the parade in '83, the work ethic and grit I watched her display daily would only quietly be admired by her oldest child.

She didn't play sports. She played the game of life—up and out of the house every morning by 4:30 a.m., in rain, sleet or snow. Making beds, vacuuming floors, cleaning toilets with a sense of purpose that only a mother could deliver. My mother was my life idol. Dr. J was my basketball idol. And all the aforementioned Philly guards were next in line.

Basketball was growing and more games were being televised. The more television coverage the NBA received, the more opportunities I had to see the creativity of others. The League's growth allowed me to see Isiah Lord Thomas dance on a basketball court. Dr. J retired and "Zeek from Chicago" stepped right in and kept me loving the game. I tried to dribble like him, I wore my socks the same length as him, I even wore my shorts high like him —- well, all of us wore our shorts high back in 1987. A kid from North Philly abruptly changed his allegiance. Isiah made me a Bad Boy Fan without me ever visiting Motor City. As a matter of fact, I could count on both hands and feet how many times I had been inside of an automobile up until that point in my life. Deeeee-Troit Basketball was ringing loud in North Philly because of my new idol, Isiah Lord Thomas.

From 1994 to 2015, Isiah Thomas reigned as my idol. And although that time span covered my collegiate and professional playing career, I still viewed him as my favorite player. But by the end of the 2015-16 NBA season, he would be removed from that position. And not because of any wrongdoing of his own, or because of a post-career evaluation of his skill set. Sports always possesses nostalgic comparisons that help illuminate every barbershop in the hood. Who is/ was a better? What team is/ was better? Could James Harden score like he does today if he had to play against the Bad Boys? Was the' 96 Bulls a better team than the 73-wins Warriors team? Russell or Chamberlain? James or Jordan? Does Kobe make it into the conversation? Curry or Magic? Cousy or Stockton? Bird, Parrish, McHale, or Duncan, Ginobili, Parker—which trio was better?

I've heard someone say, "Comparison is the thief of joy." I think that statement is true anytime we thrust ourselves or our thoughts into the equation. But when you're talking about sports, it's how we apply our perspective to validate someone or some teams' significance. Relative time is the equalizer, and the separator. So we'll never know if Kareem could guard Shaq, or if The Big O's triple doubles were more meaningful than Westbrook's. Plus, when you talk to passionate fans who are blinded by their own bias, you get outrageous statements like the forthcoming. Like, to me, Nick Foles is the greatest NFL quarterback ever! Outside of the City of Philadelphia, every NFL fan would call me crazy for making such a statement. But he delivered our city's first Super Bowl. So to me, he's better than Jaworski, Cunningham, McNabb, Manning, Brady and Montana, combined.

CHAPTER 4

EYE-TEE

In 2015, Isiah from Chicago was replaced by Isaiah from Tacoma. This Isaiah possessed membership in the 5'9" club. This Isaiah possessed membership in the All-Star selection club. This Isaiah possessed membership in the double-figure career scoring average club. He's the only player 5-foot-9 or shorter to be voted to multiple All-Star Games. He was traded to Boston Feb. 19, 2015. I didn't join the Celtics coaching staff until July of that same year. But, for two seasons, I had a floor seat every night to watch him play with physical prowess. His will and skill accented the chip he carried for being the last selection of the 2011 NBA draft. The 2015-16 season was Isaiah's coming out party. He became America's Hero—all 5-foot-9 of him.

He had the perfect combination of humility and confidence. I guess that's the definition of swag. I watched No. 4 jerseys populate NBA arenas in real time. Maybe it was his smile, maybe it was his toughness, maybe it was his skill, or maybe it was the vertical challenge he defied that made so many love him. He averaged 22.2 points and 6.2 assists that season—and went on to earn his first All-Star selection. The following season he increased his scoring average by 7 points, was selected to his second All-Star game and led the Celtics to a first-place finish during the regular season. He was 5-foot-9 and averaged 29 points per game—AMAZING.

But I wasn't surprised. I watched him prepare. Everyday. Every road trip. Every game. He had to be the first one on the floor. Rep after rep after rep. Once the team plane landed in a city, the first thing he had to do was find a gym to shoot. In all my years associated with the NBA, I never witnessed that. If the team plane landed at 5 p.m., someone from the organization had to have a gym ready. Not sometimes, not on days when he felt good, not on days that followed bad shooting nights, but every time. Pre-All-Star selection, post-All-Star selection, Isaiah would pay for his own Ubers so he could be first on the floor on game days. He had this "thing" about other people shooting at the same basket. I guess all the great ones have a "thing." Whether it drives them or calms their spirit, the great ones possess a quirkiness about their routine that helps them find their brilliance. So I had the pleasure of passing, the pleasure of serving, the pleasure of observing, truly one of the greatest athletes in the history of sports—a 5-foot-9 killa from Tacoma, Washington, named Isaiah Jamar Thomas.

We finished first in the Eastern Conference in 2016-17. We beat the Chicago Bulls in the first Round of the playoffs. We would go on to face the Washington Wizards in the 2017 Eastern Conference Semifinals. The series would go seven games, with neither team winning on the opponents' home floor. In Game Two of that series, Isaiah scored 53 points—with 29 of the 53 coming in the fourth quarter and overtime. It was a grueling series. The intensity, physicality, and attention this series carried stemmed from the heated battles during the regular season. Counting the playoffs, we played Washington 11 times that year. Many were starting to think the Celtics–Wizards matchup was turning into an interconference rivalry. In-game trash talking, social media commentary, and just plain ole competitive juices forced each regular season game to have playoff-like intensity. The first two meetings of the regular season were split, with each team winning on its home floor.

On Jan. 24, 2017, in the third meeting between the two teams, the Wizards beat the Celtics 123-108. During that game, cameras would capture a heated exchange on the bench between myself and one of the players. I was totally out of line. As a staff, we talked all the time about modeling the proper temperament—and quickly, I'd lost sight of that. Good plays, bad plays, Coach Stevens always challenged both players and coaches to move onto the next play. This exchange would be captured from every angle. So much so that, immediately following the game, my oldest son, who took Amtrak earlier in the day from Philly to attend the game, informed me that I was "trending" on Twitter. I asked him what "trending" means. Appearing severely annoyed, he looked up from his mobile device long enough to give me the "are you kidding me" look. I didn't know what trending on social media meant until he and I walked from the Verizon Center in Washington, DC, to Union Station.

I didn't take the team's postgame flight back to Boston. I had a meeting the next morning with the Camden City School District Superintendent. So Jerome II and I were walking to the Megabus when I was informed that the entire world witnessed the back and forth between Marcus Smart and I. The loss of the game, compounded with that captured exchange, made a bad night even worse. No family wants their differences aired out in public. Like any family that spends a significant amount of time together, there will be differences. But both publicly and privately, we take pride in conducting ourselves with composure and dignity. Volume and aggression aren't it. Understanding, humility, and thinking of others first—they form the staple that holds the group together. ESPN's Get Up show would make the dispute one of its headlines the following morning. To be honest though, initially, I was caught in the middle. Part of me wanted to celebrate my reflexes for standing in the exchange with North Philly posture. On the other hand, I had a greater responsibility, far greater than my ego, which required me to model the right disposition when facing conflict.

CHAPTER 5

ELEMENTS OF EXPOSURE

Jerome II and I took the Megabus from DC back to Philly. As the video clip of my spirited courtside exchange with Marcus Smart continued to trend on social media, both our phones blew up with incoming messages. It seemed like half our contacts wanted to text or talk about that moment in time. An hour into the trip, I put my phone on silent, laid down in the aisle of the lower deck, and closed my eyes. After playing pro ball in Europe for 11 years, I was used to sleeping on the floor of a bus. We arrived at 30th St. Station at 2 a.m. and walked to Jerome's apartment. I set my alarm for 5:30 a.m.

We laughed at the amount of attention the dispute continued to receive, and he told me that only his dad would sleep on the floor of a Megabus. I said there's only one Pooh Allen. He shook his head, laughed, and said, "You are right about that." I thanked him for coming to the game. I told him I loved him. Then I closed my eyes.

I was up and dressed by 6:15 a.m. so I could Uber from Jerome's apartment to my 8 a.m. meeting with the Superintendent of the Camden, New Jersey School District. We had previously partnered with School Based Youth Services (SBYS) and the director of that program helped to set up this meeting with the District. Its purpose was to recap the targeted outcomes of our Adolescent Father's Initiative.

Jerome and I co-founded JBA Advisors. Vedette Gavin and John Matthew Borders IV, a Dorchester, Massachusetts, native, helped us take the Adolescent Father's Initiative to another level. Never did we expect Sheila Johnson Fellows of the Harvard Kennedy School of Government to add to the cultural capital of the young men we were attempting to serve.

The first iteration of our Adolescent Father's Initiative had just been completed. High school students from Camden High and Strawberry Mansion Promise Academy in Philadelphia took Financial Literacy classes Saturday mornings at the Wharton School of Business. And twice a week they participated in Cognitive Behavior Training (CBT)—a six-week immersion course centered on exposure and thought. We felt by peeling back the layers of thought as it pertained to decision-making patterns, we could not only meet students where they were, but also deliver sustainable impact.

From an exposure standpoint, we also organized a visit for these students to Harvard University. There, they participated in seminars with men of color who didn't come from "access." The Harvard men were Ph.D. students, medical students, undergrads, and Kennedy School of Government Fellows. Our group was able to hear about challenging journeys that produce perseverance. Their academic paths had often been nontraditional. One had been homeless at one point in his life. Another first attended community college. One of them dropped out of college and worked as a janitor. One even had a GED. All represented hope and resilience. All would show our group that if they could make it to Harvard, so could our young men.

I think the Superintendent wanted to hear, directly from the source, why I took such an interest in a population that quite honestly, has been ignored and underserved by the rest of the world. My response was simply, "Because I am one of them." I was 22 and fresh out of college when the twins were born. And I didn't have a clue. So I was well aware of the challenges these young men were facing as high school dads. Therefore, I was willing to leverage platforms and exhaust personal resources to help push someone else forward. It was done for me and I was committed to paying it forward. Certified CBT facilitators, business classes at Wharton, identity seminars at Harvard, Community Engagement sessions with Catalyst IV Change—we were determined to exhaust every element of exposure to deliver sustainable outcomes.

The importance of this meeting is the reason I didn't fly back with the team after the Wizards game. But I needed to get to Boston because we had a back to back with Houston. Tipoff for our game was at 7:30 p.m. later that night; but first, I had this one opportunity to prove to the Superintendent that I was serious and committed. The Director of SBYS had taken a chance on us. She was guarded and protective because many have done our youth a disservice. She allowed me to show her who I truly was. In being faithful and committed, I was able to gain her trust. And in doing so, she walked me through the front door of the Camden City School District.

Our meeting concluded at 9:45 a.m. I raced out of the building and jumped into another Uber. This time my destination was the Philadelphia International Airport. I had an 11:15 a.m. flight scheduled to depart for Boston.

We arrived in Boston and I jumped into my third Uber of the day. If I didn't have enough time to go home, would I repeat the suit I wore the night before in DC? My internal debate however, focused on my dress shirt and tie. Would anyone notice if I wore the same suit? Who cared? The fans weren't coming to see me anyway. I updated my final Uber destination—100 Legends Way, TD Garden.

The team had a bad taste in its mouth from the Wizards loss. But because of the back to back NBA game schedule, they could quickly redeem themselves. TD Garden sits over top of Boston's North Station. Normally, I would arrive at 3:30 p.m. for a 7:30 p.m. tip, but since I was coming from the airport, and traffic is unpredictable in Boston, I just went straight to the arena.

I walked in the executive entrance and hurried up the back stairs to the third floor. I opened the door and walked down the familiar hallway. Its walls are covered with the nostalgia of Boston Celtics greats —Russell, Havlicek, DJ, Cousy, Red with the cigar. All these figures appear as if they are standing in the hallway, and not painted on the walls. The stories, the championships—history crowds the hallway. Photos that carry so much life slow down hurried foot traffic. I always peeked at the walls because with every home game I carried a certain amount of disbelief associated with the privilege of coaching in the NBA.

On this day, the hallway held more people than normal. At the end of the 90-foot museum, stood two figures I didn't recognize. I initially thought they might be part of the Houston Rockets' security detail. As I got further down the hall and closer to the locker room, there was something about these two that wouldn't allow me to take my eyes off them. I kept the traditional grateful expression on my face—smiling at and speaking to everyone I encountered. I reached for the door knob, smiled and greeted the unknown man and woman. Just as I was about to walk into the locker room, the man said, "Excuse me, are you Jerome Allen?" I said, "Yes." Then he stated his name and the name of the person standing next to him. Both names were preceded by the word Agent. Both individuals simultaneously produced badges and photo IDs.

Wait a minute—I just got off the plane, just got out of an Uber, just walked into TD Garden. The entire Uber ride, I was thinking about how we were going to contain James Harden—hands back and run him off the 3-point line. Two's won't beat you. And now, as I'm about to walk into the coaches' locker room, instead of Harden, I'm thinking, "Why in the hell is the FBI at my job?"

CHAPTER 6

LUKE 12:2

"For there is nothing covered that will not be revealed, nor hidden that will not be known."

The largest genre of music today is hip-hop. Never in his wildest dreams could Clive Campbell, aka DJ Kool Herc, have thought that looping breakbeats would turn into such a staple in American culture. Today, hip-hop is connected to every social norm in the world, and America is at the center of its exportation. The entire world, because of technology, can now consume cultures and experiences without ever having to physically occupy the same spaces as its creators. YouTube, Instagram, Tik Tok, and every other social media platform, allow experiences to be exported to the world. And as a result, hip-hop has grown.

Music is important. People need music. It's the most sophisticated, yet purest form of all the arts. It covers the full spectrum of emotion. It has made me cry. And it has made me rave. Every time I watch the movie "Cooley High" tears flow from my eyes the second G. C. Cameron begins to sing "It's So Hard To Say Goodbye To Yesterday." And the minute anyone from Philly hears Robert Rihmeek Williams utter these nine words, they jump out of their seats—"Ain't This What They Been Waiting For, You Ready?"

I'm from the '90s, when hip-hop was dominated by lyricists. Wordplay and storytelling captivated me. At 10 years old, my youngest son, Roman, gravitates to catchy hooks and dance craze rap. We go back and forth quite often about the best rappers of all time. I introduced him to Chuck D, KRS-One, Big Daddy Kane, Kool G Rap, Rakim, LL Cool J, EST, Biggie, and Jay-Z. He introduced me to DaBaby. One morning, I was driving him to school and "Between the Sheets" by the Isley Brothers was smoothly exiting the car speakers. He said to me, "Dad, they are using Biggie's beat." I had to correct him, "No Roman, it's the other way around." He was confused. Then I gave him a quick lesson: Brownstone and Tory Lanez, Ciara and Saweetie, Lauryn Hill and Drake. I wanted to go all the way back to Chic and the Sugar Hill Gang, but I definitely would have lost him. Actually, he was lost the moment I said something about Drake. He wouldn't even let me finish my explanation of sampling and the beauty of sound.

In defense of Drake, Roman inhaled a bunch of air and puffed his chest out like Claude did in the movie "Life." It took some convincing, but I respectfully had to bring to his attention that Drake will never be as great of an MC as Jay-Z. I had to tell him I didn't care how many people uploaded their "In My Feelings" Challenge. I told him I like Drake, and that I've even attended a Drake concert. I acknowledged that Drake touches all the stylistic avenues of the art—he has punchlines, he touches the trap, he has R&B influenced joints, he's done it all.

But I just like what I like. I stay in my lane, and at 47, although I'm not stuck in the '90s, I just like artists who deliver punchlines. And most of the guys I like lose 90% of the population when it's executed. I told him, Jadakiss, Fabolous and J. Cole are the only current artists that force me to sit still and listen. He then asked, "What about Lil somebody?" I then immediately switched the subject to school. "Roman, did you finish your homework?" Me arguing with a 10-year-old about who's the best rapper today makes no sense at all.

Again, I grew up during the '90s when Biggie and Jay-Z were lyrically unmatched. No song displayed their lyrical genius more than "Brooklyn's Finest." The similes and metaphors they used captured so much. Their range in flow displayed the full spectrum of the art. Whether it was Jay executing perfect delivery over Broadway's "Hard Knock Life" or Biggie killing Diana Ross' disco-influenced, "I'm Coming Out," they both did it to perfection. "Big Pimpin'" and "Notorious Thugs" were two songs with beats designed for the other featured artists on the tracks. Jay switched flows to blend in with the southern drawl of UGK. And Biggie sped up the cadence to match the pace of "Bone Thugs-N-Harmony." Neither artist lost integrity—both remained true to themselves.

I'm the same age as hip-hop, and in all my years of living and breathing the culture, no two artists have had better storytelling abilities than Big and Jay. "One More Chance" (Remix), "Story To Tell," and "Warning" are three of Biggie's classics. He painted the atmosphere so well that the listener walked through the experience wearing virtual reality goggles. He made me want to go to the club and buy Moet. I was reminded of the cold in my eye every time I wake up in the morning. He embraced his self-proclaimed physical flaws by penning, "Heart throb, never, black and ugly as ever." But finished it with one word: "However."

Someone might say it's subjective and that there's no true metric out there to determine which era and which artist should reign as the best ever. Like sports, great debates exist in other art realms also. The window for sustained excellence has an expiration date in basketball. And although there isn't an athleticism clock attached to a rapper's career, those that study the culture may say rappers have a shelf life as well. I'm not quite sure which one is shorter, the career of a professional athlete or the career of a rapper. The only thing I am sure of is that, at the age of 50, Jay-Z remains relevant both culturally and lyrically. His music catalog is too vast for me to pick out favorites. His career covers over two decades—over two decades at the top. I'd be disrespecting the full body of work if I pulled out two or three tracks. But if you want to get a 2- minute glimpse into the indescribable, just listen to "A Dream." I really thought he had that conversation with Big.

So hip-hop, the art, covered my neighborhood long before it covered the BillBoards. I connected with it lyrically and culturally. It gave color to a gloomy place, while simultaneously building out a community. It let me know my sense of normalcy was common and my dreams were common. It gave me hope and a sense of pride. It delivered and exposed. The art, the wordplay, created a new language. The expression created fashion trends. I begged my mom for a pair of Shell Toe Adidas. And rocked them with no shoestrings in them (never thinking that it would be impossible to walk if the shoes weren't laced up).

Hip-hop gave me confidence. It educated me and it made me move. I wanted others to move so I started deejaying. My life is a perfect blend of two tracks. The beats per minute don't always sync, but scratch techniques and loops have allowed the tracks of my life to hold whatever flow God chooses to spit. I owe a lot to hip-hop. It even inspired the title of this book. And because of hip-hop, I knew that having The Alphabet show up at my job couldn't be a good thing.

CHAPTER 7

LOOSE DOGS

Have you ever got caught off guard, rattled or ran down on? Like turning the corner in the hood and a loose, unchained dog is staring you in the eyes? There's a subtle moment of paralysis that buys you enough time (probably a millisecond) to calculate the quickest exit plan. It's either take off running or hop on top of the nearest car. Dogs in the hood were mean and trained to attack. For your house, they were the unofficial alarm system. The sign, "Beware of Dog" was deterrent propaganda. Behind it followed a starving bark. There weren't too many lap dogs in the hood when I was growing up. No short hair Chihuahuas, or teacup Yorkies. Only German shepherds, pit bulls, Rottweilers, and Doberman pinschers. Forget today's version of home protection, our version of the Ring walked on all fours.

In my neighborhood, we called them The Alphabet Boys—any branch of law enforcement that could be represented in acronym form. The FBI, the DEA, the DOJ, heck even the IRS, all posed as intimidating figures in the hood. Imagine turning the corner, and unexpectedly one of those aforementioned hood home protection devices was drooling at the mouth in front of you. That's the same state of paralysis I felt when I heard The Alphabet first announce themselves. Triggers and defensiveness go hand in hand. See a stray dog, run. Get approached by The Alphabet, be defensive—even if you don't have anything to be defensive about. So I thought. I was defensive and clueless. Skeptical, but certain. Unsure, but confident. None of it made sense, until they hit me with their opening question.

Should I call my lawyer? Do I even have a lawyer on retainer? I wasn't anticipating any heat. My natural guard was up, but that's just the nature of my posture in certain situations. Like, I always glance at a cop car anytime I pass one. Doesn't make sense, but I do. I'm doing the speed limit, I don't have anything to hide or be worried about—but it's something about my posture, my pigment, that goes on alert anytime our paths cross. Some may not understand, some may relate. Either way, it's a perspective that has turned out to carry living significance as of late.

I sat in the chair, upright, shoulders back, as if I was a customer service agent or a concierge. Confident with nothing to hide, I answered the first question. By the third question my eyes began to squint, and hand movements accompanied every response. The lag time between question and response started to increase as the number of questions increased. "Mr. Allen, could you verify this document for us? You're not the target, but we're looking for some clarity." Were they trying to get me to relax and be less calculated? I don't know. But after hearing that statement, I knew I was in trouble. My grandmother used to always say, "What's done in the dark will always come to light."

PART II

Well, maybe you're just a chip off the old block, Ray.
CLAUDE BANKS, *Life*

CHAPTER 8

HAND-PICKED: THE EIGHTH SON

Like David, I too, was hand-picked. We all know the story of David and Goliath. It's been the victory chant of many in the sports world. Society, in its normalcy, uses David's triumph as empirical evidence to prove that anything is possible—the underdog will always have a chance. David's victory delivers the necessary amount of hope anytime an opponent faces steep opposition. The melody of their original battle still touches our heartstrings today. Whether it's UMBC's victory over No. 1 seed UVA in the 2018 Men's NCAA Basketball Tournament, or Buster Douglas' 11th round knockout of then Heavyweight Champion, Mike Tyson, the shock of the result always gives reference to David's victory over Goliath.

David, the shepherd, the eighth son of Jesse, would eventually go on to be King of Israel and author countless Psalms. His existence before the epic battle with Goliath possessed nothing of importance to the periphery. The world judged his significance by stature, by position, by job title. In those days being a shepherd was slightly above the social irrelevance of a slave. But God saw him differently from man. When the priest, prophet and judge Samuel was sent to David's father house to anoint the next king of Israel, David's father brought out seven sons before he reluctantly requested the appearance of the eighth and final one. Samuel saw Jesse's first son and was sure he was God's choice. He fit the world's description of King's imagery—tall, handsome, well-built. It was his outward appearance that resonated with Samuel: he reminded Samuel of the previous King.

We all do it—we stay within the familiar, we are copycats, we get used to it, and or become comfortable, even when the person in leadership is ineffective. We bind ourselves to a supposed process and deem it to be exact. Whether it's a look, a particular background, a job title—we all calculate the validity of someone else's right to be elevated based on years of service or association. It's mankind's way of controlling the process, no matter how wrong or outdated it may be. In David's day, birth order, stature, and job title determined your social value. But God didn't follow man-made metrics. God knew David wasn't perfect. But He knew that David was a man after His own heart.

God's selection of Israel's next King wasn't led by the power of the eye. God saw something inside of David —something that only He could see. Man would have chosen someone else. Sometimes people can see things in you that you can't see in yourself. My wife would echo those words to me on numerous occasions. God saw David's heart, and as a result, He hand-picked Jesse's eighth son to be the next king of Israel.

CHAPTER 9

HAND-PICKED: THE VOLUNTEER

The Ivy League allows its basketball coaching staff to have three assistant coach positions. Two of the slots are paid positions, and one coach carries a volunteer tag. That means no salary and no benefits. In the past, many coaches who fell into the volunteer spot usually found outside sources of income. If you're married and have kids, this position is a tough one to manage. The demands of the job, coupled with the demands of having a family, stretch you at both ends. The "only two paid positions" baffles me. How can you ask a coach to perform all the duties of the other coaches, be at practice, recruit, prepare scouts, be an integral part of pushing the program forward, exhaust themselves—yet not be able to compensate them? And God forbid his or her child gets sick, they can't even take them to the emergency room because the position doesn't offer health benefits.

The University of Pennsylvania does not offer athletic scholarships. As staff, we were charged with beating scholarship schools, which required our entire staff to spread out and grind. We had to cover the entire country, and sometimes the world. Now I'm asking a coach (who doesn't get paid to begin with) to come out of his or her pocket, purchase flights, book hotels, rent cars and then wait three to six weeks to get reimbursed. And, by the way, please don't lose a receipt, because if you do, you'll have to eat the cost of the expense.

What I found out after coaching at both the collegiate and professional level, is that people really pay close attention to tiers. This guy is the associate head coach, and that guy is the first assistant, or second assistant. This guy sits on the front of the bench, and that guy is player development. Every position has a supposed valuation assigned to it. Both levels have insecurities associated with an industry that, unfortunately, is consistent with how society calculates significance. I remember being on the road recruiting in college as both an assistant coach and as a head coach. As an assistant, certain guys who worked at certain levels would determine whether you were worthy enough to greet based on the name embroidered on your polo shirt. I've had this happen to me on many occasions, and there is one story I'll never forget.

Traveling on the road as a 37-year-old head coach, I switched in and out of dress code. Some schools mandated that you always represented their university in posture and attire. In college there's the traditional "coaches-look" (slacks/ khakis and a sweater or short sleeve university stitched polo). I didn't require the staff to wear any of the above. They were men, they knew, based on the relationship and the setting, what was appropriate and what was not. My one requirement was that they be comfortable. So slacks, jeans, sneakers, loafers, sweats, and or suits were all in play. Distance and means of transportation usually determined how I dressed. If I was doing a home visit, I normally wore a suit and tie. If I was going to a local high school game and I had a preexisting relationship with the high school coach, I could wear sweats or khakis. For five-hour car rides, same thing. When I had to get on an airplane, I usually went one of two ways: jeans, Jordans and a backpack, or slacks and a sweater. I was 37–38 years old and not too far removed from my playing days, so I still had my Jordan shoe collection in the garage. I wore skinny jeans. As a matter of fact, I have been wearing skinny jeans since the year 2000, ever since I went to my first soccer derby —- Roma vs Lazio in Olympia Stadium in Rome, Italy. That atmosphere, that country, not only changed my outlook on life, it changed my wardrobe as well. I went from one end of the spectrum to the other. Living in Italy made me trade in my 4X white tees and oversized jeans for fitted Gucci shirts and skinny jeans.

In 2010, the slim fitted look was just starting to be a staple in American culture. I had 10 years in with the style by the time I started taking college recruiting trips. One day I took a recruiting trip to Oklahoma City. Again, as a staff, we could no longer stay in the tri-state area to recruit. There were two high school seniors who popped up on our radar. Teammates, getting mid major interest, who mirrored an Ivy League academic profile—we had to go lay eyes on them.

Wearing skinny jeans, Jordans and a light UPenn windbreaker, I exited the plane, jumped in a rent-a-car and headed to the school. I had never spoken to the head coach of the school; one of our other coaches did. I was pretty certain he informed the school that Coach Allen was coming. High school coaches get blind calls on players all the time, so I didn't expect him to remember the call. I never led with my title, and I never said I was anyone's boss. They were my co-workers; they were my peers. We were all men, with families and responsibilities. I made sure they knew no position or title would make me more important than them. We had a job to do and we were going to get it done together.

Anyway, I drove to the school, walked into the gym and stood and watched the open run. No other college coach was present at this particular workout. I politely introduced myself to the other three gentlemen in the gym: the head coach of the boys' team, an assistant coach and one of his friends. For 45 minutes, I stood and watched the open run. Usually if it's my first time observing a prospective student/athlete, I like to watch as much of the workout as I can. If I've seen a kid multiple times, I'd fraternize with whoever's in attendance. Those types of visits happen when I'm just going to show love, not evaluate. But with this being my first trip to Oklahoma City, I'm watching everything they do. Do they play defense, do they communicate, do they celebrate their teammates, are they getting back in transition, can they handle the ball, are they physical, do they compete or complain? I watched game after game after game.

Finally, there's stoppage in play because of an injury. So the head coach walks over to me and says, "Ay Coach, what school are you from, again?" I say, "The University of Pennsylvania." He says, "That's right, Penn State." I say, "No, UPenn and Penn State are two different schools —like OU and OSU."

He says, "So what conference are y'all in?" I say, "The Ivy League-Harvard, Princeton, Yale, etc." He says, "Is that D1?" I say, "Yes." He then says "OK," and walks away.

Ten minutes later, he walks back over to where I had been standing for 55 minutes and says, "Ay, yo, Coach, what's y'all head coach name, again?" I say, "Jerome Allen." He says, "Oh." He then proceeds to ask, how long has Jerome been the head coach there and how long have I been there as well. I tell him, "I've been there the same amount of time." He says, ``Coach, tell me your name again?" I say, "Jerome Allen." He says, "No, what's your name?" I say, "Jerome Allen."

He says, "Wait—you Jerome Allen, the head coach?" I say, "Yes." He says, "You the head coach?" I say, "Yes." Then he turns around to the other two guys sitting in the corner of the gym and says, "Mannnnn, somebody get this man a chair."

I shake my head and said, "Naw, I'm cool standing."

In my head, I was saying to myself, "Man, I wonder if he would have even acknowledged my existence when I was the volunteer assistant?"

When I was an undergrad at UPenn, post-practice meals were always consumed at the T-House, the closest dining hall to all the athletic facilities. It actually was connected to the nation's first two-tier football stadium, Franklin Field. Today the T-House poses as the Dunning Coaches Center. Its second and third floor contain office space for 18 different varsity sports. From Lightweight Crew to Field Hockey, most of Penn's coaching prowess is housed in the Dunning Coaches Center. We were a tight group, as evidenced by our legendary Christmas parties. We supported and challenged one another. And our departmental dysfunction registered significantly lower than that of a normal family. Head Coaches, Assistant Coaches, Volunteer Coaches—all occupied the most eastern part of campus, with pride and togetherness.

Men's and Women's Basketball shared a suite. It was by far the biggest coaches' suite in the entire building. Our Director of Basketball Operations (DBO) desk split the room in half. Women's Basketball on the left and Men's Basketball on the right. Directly behind the DBO's desk were two desks facing opposite walls. Depending on which side of the room you were on, a bay window provided natural light. The two desks made its occupants sit with their backs to one another. Anyone who entered the basketball suite could see if someone was seated at the desks that faced the wall.

This space was reserved for the Volunteer Assistants—in the back, facing the wall, being seen but not heard. If you were lucky enough, the foot traffic courted by the basketball suite would occasionally acknowledge your existence. Most of the time, however, you were ignored. People would stroll into the suite and not even bat an eyelid toward the Volunteers. If, as a Volunteer Assistant Coach, I didn't initiate the greeting, the foot traffic would head directly to the desired office.

To this day, I always speak to, or acknowledge everyone anytime I walk into a new space. Whether it be the office, the court or the house, you'll never be the first to speak. It drove me crazy. They could see me before I could see them because my desk faced the wall. But my job title, my position in the room, would determine whether or not I would be acknowledged. What I've found out, though, is that the same dynamic occurs no matter what setting you're in. People gravitate to positions, titles, stature. One common element in human existence is that, at our core, we only desire to be acknowledged. Yet many are calculated and misled by the eye. The power of the eye creates an overlooked pool. And if any in the overlooked pool possess high doses of insecurity, shrinkage enters their posture. Or worse, they adopt loud volume, in an attempt to draw attention to themselves.

I sat in the back of the basketball suite, boiling inside, but determined not to allow others to define my significance. I just wanted to help, to serve, to push the program forward. And along the way, receive just a slight bit of acknowledgement. I mean, I did play at the school. I was a part of the brotherhood. But nothing! If it wasn't someone entering the suite because they were specifically looking for me, or there wasn't a preexisting relationship, most of the time, I, the Volunteer Assistant, was invisible. They came seeking others.

CHAPTER 10

HAND-PICKED:
THE INTOXICATION OF SELF

After a 0-7 start to the Quakers' 2009-10 season, the University's athletic director sought to make a coaching change. Most coaching changes that happen in-season usually solicit the services of an assistant. The pecking order traditionally goes associate head coach, first assistant, then volunteer assistant. It's the standard tier system used by the industry. From the amount of game tickets and location of seats to salary, most athletic departments distribute additional compensation based on years of service and or title.

The AD was in a tough spot. However, he decided not to wait until the end of the season to make a change. He was going to do it right away. In his mind, winter break was soon approaching, and with a pause in the game schedule, due to exams, the new/interim coach would have at least two weeks to re-galvanize the squad.

The current Associate Head Coach had been an assistant for 11 years, at four different schools. The First Assistant had five years of service as a Division 1 coach. And the Volunteer had been coaching for three months. Once rumors started to circulate that the AD was going to make a change, everybody had either a theory, or an opinion. Coaching trees, former players who now coach, head coaches at other institutions—everyone chimed in on the potential coaching vacancy while we still had a coach in place. Six years later, I would find out for myself how it feels to be in that position. To be coaching while rumors circulate about the position you currently hold can be maddening. It's a lot easier to "resist the noise" in theory.

Samuel walked into Jesse's house and figuratively, Penn's AD walked into the basketball suite. God told Samuel not to look with the eyes of man. The AD didn't evaluate his candidates based on industry standards. Was Jesse's oldest son supposed to be the selection because of his birthright? Was the associate head supposed to be elevated because of his title? God hand-picked David, the same way the AD hand-picked me, the volunteer. I did nothing to merit the elevation. But yet I would soon hold the dream position with such an excessive amount of entitlement. So much so that I forgot I was gifted the position to begin with.

Have you ever driven a car and the wheel alignment was off? Or drove a car that didn't have power steering? Today, with all the technological advances in the car industry, self- driving cars make my power steering question sound ridiculous. But just like a car, life becomes more difficult to navigate when you're out of alignment. It gives you amnesia—you forget your own story, and consequently open doors to significant collateral damage. When you are out of alignment, you forget the fact that you were hand-picked. The shepherd, the last son, became King of Israel. The volunteer, the ignored, became Head Coach. The irony in David's story, however, is that the place where he had his greatest victory would also be the same place where he would have his greatest failure. A war helped him walk into his purpose. His defeat of Goliath benchmarked the beginning of a stellar career as a warrior. David the king, was David the warrior first. His entire reign, he led from the front. If there was a battle to be fought, King David was present. But the day when he wasn't where he was supposed to be, when he was out of alignment, he exposed himself to pitfalls that had generational ramifications.

Had he been at war with his army, he might have never exposed himself to the consequences associated with adultery and murder. Others would be impacted as well. However, the shepherd, the hand-picked King, who committed adultery and murder, would still be greatly used by God. He would go on to pen a total of 73 Psalms. "The Lord is my shepherd," starts Psalm 23. David penned that.

Had the hand-picked Head Coach been at practice, or at a game, or allowed University processes and procedures to play out as they were designed—simply put, had he operated in harmony with his platform, his position, he would not be penning this story as a convicted felon. Will this be his story, or only part of his story? Although his failure in character has had life-altering consequences, he holds onto the hope that his life will possess significance.

The gratefulness toward being hand-picked faded as time passed. The further I got away from the initial elevation, the more I operated in my own strength. And the more I operated in my own strength, the further I got out of alignment. Instead of following our normal student athlete recruiting model, I elected to deviate from industry practices. It became more about me and less about service. The burdens I was attempting to address still needed to be serviced, but not by the means in which I was attempting to do so. Not by cutting deals under the table.

Being hand-picked is something you never lose sight of—gratefulness should always consume the body. Lines don't get blurred, and processes and procedures don't get ignored. How could the volunteer assistant, who became head coach after only having three months of experience be so bothered, be so annoyed, be so arrogant, be so impatient, be so ignorant, be so selfish, be so stupid? God's swiftness and acceleration couldn't be mirrored by a Disney script. But the intoxication of self and the disease of More will cause even the hand-picked to have lapses in judgement.

CHAPTER 11

MITCH AND JOE

Coming out of Episcopal Academy, I was awarded the Mayor's Scholarship to the University of Pennsylvania. Residency, along with acceptance into the school, determined whether this particular scholarship could be assigned to persons. There were other factors as well that supported qualification. First generation college students, students from single-parent homes, or students that didn't come from "access," could apply for the scholarship. Don't quote me, but, years ago, in exchange for City-owned land and control of particular urban space, the University agreed to establish this academic partnership. If you fit the academic criteria for acceptance, and you lived in the City of Philadelphia, and you checked any of the socio-economic boxes, you could potentially be awarded the Mayor's Scholarship. The partnership was a win-win for both the City and the University. It would create a diverse body of higher learning, and ultimately deliver more citizens of the world. The more diverse, the more perspectives, the more cultural relevance a space engulfs, the more informed its constituents will be. University officials and City officials would perfectly execute this, with the establishment of the Philadelphia Mayor's Scholarship.

This scholarship made tuition to the University free. Room, board, miscellaneous fees, would still be considered a cost to the student and his or her family. I had to take out loans to cover the additional cost associated with attending Penn. Today, the nation's 7th wealthiest school, with an endowment of $14 billion dollars, has a financial aid policy strikingly different from when I attended the University as an undergrad. All of today's financial aid reads are strictly based on need. The financial aid packages are covered by the award and grants. No longer are loans required through the University to support and close the gap. It's all need based. But in 1991, that wasn't the case. There was a significant gap that wasn't covered by the Mayor's Scholarship. Out of all the colleges interested in me when I was coming out of high school, I chose the one school that didn't offer a full athletic scholarship.

I had 16 Division I offers. Schools from major conferences came to my grandparents' house and attempted to highlight the brilliance of their respective programs. I had ACC offers, Big East offers, Atlantic 10 offers and MEAC offers. I had scholarship offers in two different sports—11 for basketball and five for football. All for free, with no financial burden to my mother and I. But I decided to go to the one school that didn't offer athletic scholarships. And I would have to take out loans in order to attend.

Now, I'd be lying if I said to you that at the time of my decision, I knew Penn was going to change my life in ways that none of the other schools could. Some of the schools on my list were great academic institutions, but none of them compared to the Wharton School of Business at the University of Pennsylvania.

If it weren't for Mitchell Leibovitz and Joseph Pandolphi, I would not have gone to Penn. These two men helped me figure out my college decision dilemma—the 40-year decision vs the 4-year decision. Mitchell Leibovitz was the CEO of Pep Boys and Joseph Pandolphi was a private family doctor. Mitchell's son, Dan, was my friend and teammate on the basketball team at Episcopal Academy. We both started out playing JV our freshman year. Dr. P's two sons were my closest friends on the football team. Chris was a running back, Michael was the center, and I played quarterback. Both dads knew the significance of a Wharton degree. My mom couldn't weigh in on the decision. Her sense of normalcy allowed her to adopt the posture of an active, but uninformed parent. As a high school dropout who made $11,000 a year cleaning hotel rooms, she couldn't connect with the enormity of the decision.

I wanted to be an accountant. My favorite subject in school was math. And although I dreamed of playing in the NBA, my daily focus was on just getting a good job so I could take care of my mom. I didn't think the NBA was realistic, but I did think that playing college ball for one of those programs that played their games on CBS was a possibility. It was all I watched. It was all I knew. Saturday afternoon matchups between St. Johns and Georgetown, and or Pitt vs Villanova, forced me to sit still on the living room floor. I was completely oblivious to Penn's sports history and even more oblivious to the University's relevance both locally and nationally.

Dan's mom and grandfather went to Penn. His dad, Mitch, who was a bigtime Temple University alum, was pushing Penn. And my entire senior year, Dr. Pandolphi kept telling me I was going to Penn. In passing, whether at football games, or basketball games, he would whisper it. But there was something about that South Philly Italian accent that made the whisper sound directive—almost like, "Jerome,

I'm not asking you where you're going to college, I'm telling you." Man, I thank God for both of those men. They knew Penn would change the trajectory of my entire family.

CHAPTER 12

JUDGEMENT: ANALYTICS

B eing a Mayor's Scholar meant I was eligible for a work-study grant. I had to maintain full-time status as a student. And in doing so, there would be part-time employment opportunities throughout campus. The maximum number of hours a student could work weekly was twenty. Depending on the department and the job description, you could earn anywhere from minimum wage to $8 per hour. Most students worked until the amount of the work-study award was exhausted. I tried not to use up all my hours too soon. I wanted to stretch the award out over the entire school year. I would work 8 to 10 hours a week so that on weekends I could lessen the blow on my mom. In 1991, Penn's dining services were closed on the weekends. So my only on-campus eating options were McDonalds, or a cheese steak from Billy Bob's. My work-study checks would be between $50 and $70. That was enough to get a haircut, and get into the AKA party Friday night, and the Kappa party Saturday night. If my compensation for the week rendered funds closer to the $70 mark, I'd take the L train downtown and buy a Polo shirt from John Wanamaker's. My mom told me my dad used to shop at the same department store. I'd only go if I knew they were having a sale.

I generally had to decide between my head and my body. I could walk into the party with a fresh cut and an old outfit, or I could rock a new shirt and hope that it kept the attention off my head. It was one or the other. However, for major events such as Homecoming or Penn Relays, I had to have both—a new shirt and a fresh cut. That's when I would go home and sit on my grandmother's couch until my mom got home from work. I knew what day was payday, and I knew what time she got home from work. She'd walk through the door and see me sitting on the couch and start shaking her head. I'd jump up, hug her, kiss her, and tell her I loved her, with my hand out the entire time. "Mom, DJ Clue is bringing Jay-Z to Irvine Auditorium tonight. You know I gotta be there." She'd always respond, "Boy, you and this rap stuff." Then she'd give me $25 or $30 and I'd run out the door to catch the 23 trolley back to campus.

My work-study job landed me in Steinberg Dietrich Hall. It housed the Management Department for both Wharton's undergraduate and graduate professors. The Marks-Darivoff Family Professor of Management, Keith Weigelt, allowed me to record statistical data from various projects. These projects/exercises took place both in class and out of class. Keith was, and probably still is one of the smartest human beings I ever met in my life. I was a Strategic Management major at Penn. It's basically the study of small group dynamics, or human resource exploration—how groups form, operate, collaborate and optimize their collective existence for the greater good. Keith taught three of the classes I was required to take in order to declare Strategic Management as my degree concentration under the Management umbrella. Needless to say, between class and work-study, I spent a ton of time around this genius of a man.

Two things Professor Weigelt was really into were Eastern Thought and Game Theory. At first, both of these topics were a little too much for me to digest. But Prof used the greatest equalizer there was to make it all make sense. He used sports—in particular, he used the game of basketball. Prof exposed me to reading materials such as the book, "The Art of War." He used terrains and angles to talk about vision and ideal trap areas on the basketball court. He talked about the appearance of formless—having no likes or dislikes. He would equate it to being able to drive left just as well as I could drive the ball right. He told me that being formless on the court meant my jumpshot had to be just as effective as my ability to get to the basket. I wasn't considered a "jump shooter" in college. But Prof forced me to become formless, and as a result, we spent countless hours in the gym, him as the rebounder and me as the shooter. Well, actually, he didn't force me.

One day I was sitting in his office and he said he got a call from Phil Jackson. He said it so casually that it didn't even register at first that he was talking about the Phil Jackson, the coach of the Chicago Bulls. I looked at him puzzled, thinking to myself, "Why would Phil Jackson call Prof?" So I asked him what Phil wanted. He explained to me that they both have a strong interest in Eastern Thought and from time to time Phil reaches out to him. Prof had never mentioned this to me before. But I wasn't surprised. Me being a wise guy, I said, "Prof, I bet Phil's not telling Jordan he needs to be formless." Prof looked at me and said, "if you like, we can go through the data from Jordan's first three years in the NBA and compare his 3-point shooting percentages from those seasons with his 3-point shooting percentage now, and I guarantee you it's 20 percentage points higher today." I said No way.

He made me collect the data. Jordan shot 37% from 3-point range during the 1992–93 season. His percentage from the same distance from 1984–87 was 17%. We sat next to one another, staring at the data. With a smirk on his face, Prof said, "See, I told you, even Jordan wants to become formless."

The selfless job of chasing down all of my misses just so he could sew into me is something I'll never forget. His service was twofold, though. He also would talk to me about the analytics of the game. We argued all the time about what was a good shot and what was not. He took historical data and assigned a valuation to the timing and location of shots. He was all about efficiency and forming optimizing strategies based on the data. This was in 1992, when the "mid-range" jump shot was still considered a good shot in basketball. I must admit, I thought he was crazy. Today though, the analytical NBA shot models resemble that which Prof tried to get me to embrace some 28 years prior.

Professor Weigelt was ahead of his time—or maybe I was too stubborn to listen. "Analytic guys" now run a significant amount of NBA franchises. Owners understand numbers, and although players' grace and flare convince fans to spend their disposable income on entertainment in the form of sports, it's still a business. Why wouldn't an owner want to be efficient, win and make money? Most of them hold other entities as their primary source of income. Whether it be hedge funds, real estate or tech companies, many NBA owners completely understand the language of big data as it pertains to both player and efficiency. The numbers speak for themselves. However, the game isn't played in exacts. Plus, if you collect enough data, you can create or support any narrative you want. The good ones, however, use the information to support and highlight areas of the game that are important to them and their winning formula.

In 1992, Professor Weigelt argued that the ball must be passed at least three times on an offensive possession before a shot was taken. I would tell him we should take the first shot that's available, regardless of the number of passes. I'd continue by saying, "We can't play like robots and be on the floor overthinking, passing up opportunities because we haven't made three passes. We must play free." He would always go back to the game film and say, "Not only didn't the ball touch the paint, you took 70% of your shots off two passes or less, and that's why you lost." I'd get angry and say, "No, we lost because I need to play better."

In today's NBA, it's safe to say every team's offensive emphasis is to get layups, free throws and 3's. Again, Prof was ahead of his time. I was just a stubborn point guard who refused to listen to a genius. What could a management professor teach me about basketball and strategy? He never played, he's not athletic. He wears glasses and he reads books. He can't execute a pick and roll, and he can't shake a defender. How could he even fix his lips to tell me how to play the game? Many times in life we allow the optics to determine the validity of the message giver. It would be a mistake I would reference several times as I progressed in life. No longer would I allow the power of the eye to generate connectivity and or comprehension. Prof knew that big data was starting to drive corporation's decision-making patterns. And it was soon to change sports and the way its athletes displayed their grace and flair. Space, pace, five out, threes, layups, and free throws—offensive objectives and defensive strategies have changed. The game has shifted away from iso ball and post play. Contested midrange jump shots are now frowned upon.

Big data changed GMs' lenses. Big data changed coaches' player development strategies. Big data made position-specific players desire to become formless. Who would have ever thought that shot location and expected valuation would be the drivers of modern-day basketball? In 1992, I was on the groundbreaking floor of analytics and basketball. However, I was too judgmental to get past the ignorance that coated my eyes. He never played the game; therefore, I wasn't listening. Boy, was I wrong.

CHAPTER 13

JUDGEMENT: JAN. 7, 1994

The place of judgement, 235 S. 33rd Street, Philadelphia. The building, The Palestra. The word judgement carries two connotations:1) the ability to make considered decisions or come to sensible conclusions; 2) a misfortune or calamity viewed as a divine punishment. The latter is where I landed on both sides of the word. To judge and then be judged is a fascinating phenomenon. On one side, my judgement of others is an outward gesture, solely looking for a landing spot for fault. Upon close examination, one can argue that although exact offenses might not have transpired, we've all put ourselves in a position to be judged. And when it happens, do we extend the compassion and forgiveness that was lacking when we were doing the judging?

It took 44 years for me to stop being so judgmental of my father—44 years. And the only reason it happened was because I was in the position of culprit. My failure in character was so significant that its rippling effect rocked my son's world. When my dad rocked my world some 25 years prior, I vowed to hate him for the rest of my life. When I rocked my own son's world, I begged for forgiveness. One of the best things my failure in character did was expose my hypocrisy. When the judge is being judged, it forces reflection. It brings about awareness, and it acknowledges the importance of correction. Most importantly, though, it frees the captive and opens the pathway to forgiveness.

My place of judgement took place at The Palestra. Palestra means gym, in Italian. When it's referred to as such in the intercollegiate world, The Palestra is known as college basketball's most historic gymnasium. More college basketball games have been played in that arena than any other arena in the country. And proudly, it poses as the home arena for both the Men's and Women's basketball programs at the University of Pennsylvania. It holds roughly 8,722 seats — and depending on the two adversaries for an approaching contest, concrete planks, known as aisles, can boost attendance up to 8,800. Big 5 games, NCAA tournament games and Penn-Princeton rivalries, all have been graciously hosted by this iconic structure. Designed by the father of gothic educational structures, Charles Klauder, The Palestra doors first opened Jan. 1, 1927. Brad Stevens and I respectfully debated over which building was more historic, Butler's Hinkle Fieldhouse or The Palestra. And although the movie "Hoosiers" highlighted Hinkle's brilliance, nothing in this country compares to The Palestra—old structures, new structures, none captures the true essence of college basketball like The Palestra.

FRIDAY, JANUARY 7, 1994.

On this night the Quakers would go on to defeat the Crimson of Harvard 92-76. It would be one of the 14 league victories secured during the 1993–94 season. We went undefeated in league play the season before, and although our goal wasn't to duplicate that feat, we were committed to winning one game 14 times. My pregame routine was to arrive two, to two and a half hours before tipoff. I liked being on the floor by myself. Professor Weigelt's influence challenged me to visualize space and situations before they occurred. Being on the court alone gave me a chance to work on the visualization of success. If I could slow the mind down enough to think fast and play slow, I could always make optimal decisions on the basketball court. So, if someone walked into The Palestra on game day and heard a ball bouncing between 4:30 and 5 p.m., they knew the creator of the rhythmic sounds was me. If it was just the squeaky sounds made by the abrupt stoppage of shoes that meant I was channeling my inner defensive spirit.

Big 5 matchups against Temple University's Aaron Mckie, Villanova University's Alvin Williams, or LaSalle University's Kareem Townes, required my pregame exercise to be solely focused on closeout angles and ball pressure. If the off-cadence rhythm of the ball bouncing resembled the sharpness of Doug E. Fresh beatboxing, then that meant I was trying to anticipate shot locations based on our upcoming opponent's scouting report. Although we won the game that night, I wasn't locked in or focused the way I was for all of our preceding games. I was "off" as we say in the sports world. How I got there, or rather, what caused me to be "off" could be attributed to one thing, one person. And that one person was my dad.

Before I arrived at The Palestra on this Friday night,, I went to the check cashing store on 40th Street to cash my work-study check. As mentioned earlier, I usually saved my money for haircuts, parties, gear and occasional meals. But during the season, I rarely went to parties, and I wore team-issued travel sweats all weekend. This was a $70 paycheck, so I said to myself, "When I see my dad tonight after the game, I'm gonna ask him if he needs $20 or something." I was excited and feeling good about the fact that I'd be able to share my earnings with him. I thought he would probably need it. My mom received her weekly paycheck the day before, so I knew she was straight. And if she wasn't, I'd know right away because she was always the first parent to arrive at The Palestra on game days. I'd be able to see it all over her face. I mean every home game, by 5:30 p.m., she'd be planted on the last row of Section 110, ready to scream, jump, and cheer for her beloved Quakers. But this day, I was holding onto a couple of extra bucks in case my dad needed them. It's weird because prior to this day, I never thought about sharing anything I had with him. I even hated when I used to see him kiss his own wife. "That's my mom, don't put your lips on her." I was truly a momma's boy.

For 30 minutes I shot shot after shot after shot. Jump shots off the dribble, jump shots after change of direction moves, jump shots off the catch. I kept fumbling the pickup coming out of Tim Hardaway's UTEP Two Step. I kept losing Coach Fran O'Hanlon's snatch-back crossover. People in Philadelphia think I invented this move. The rest of the country thinks God Shammgod invented it. The reality of it all is that Rainbow Johnson, aka the Head Coach of Men's Basketball at Lafayette College, aka Francis O'Hanlon, showed me the move at the end of my sophomore year. And here I was, a year later, still trying to perfect the move in traffic.

I tried to steal moves from everyone I could. If you know something, or had something in your game that was effective, I always tried to add it to mine. I was a sponge—even at the age of 47 I try to steal all I can from this current group of NBA players. Not because I'm trying to add to my game; my playing days have long passed me. But more so because there's a certain element of insecurity amongst great athletes that won't allow them to use others' uniqueness. Maybe that's part of the reason why they've reached the professional level—pushing themselves and desiring to top whoever is in front of them.

So I steal only to share, trying to remove the perception of mimicking. And secretly, I also steal so that I have something to offer my 10-year-old son—who, according to him, is wayyyyyy better than the washed-up, baldheaded bum that he's forced to reference as his dad. I say to him all the time, "Roman, you know I get paid to help pros, right?" He says, "Yeah, I know, but none of them are me." That's when I throw my hands up and rest on being plain ole Dad. If anyone ever figures out how to get your own child to listen to you, could you post the receipt online for me? Please?

Soaking in sweat, walking off the floor, feeling good about my just-completed pregame work, I approached the locker room only to be stopped by our team's equipment manager.

"Jerome, does your dad need money?"

I looked at him with a frown on my face and my head tilted, Hun?"

He repeated the question, "Does your dad need money?"

Obviously annoyed by the confusing question, I said, "Jim, what are you talking about?"

Jim goes on to inform me that my dad was outside, in front of The Palestra, asking people for change as they approached the building. He was soooo high he didn't realize where he was.

Everybody knew he was my dad. How could he embarrass me like that? I couldn't believe it. I kicked the locker room door open, walked to my stall, put my face in the palm of my hands, and wept so hard that the snot and tears met right at the tip of my upper lip. The embarrassment was too much to bear. We had the same first name, I looked like a younger version of him. I was his oldest child, his only boy. Why would he do such a thing? On campus, at my school, in front of The Palestra? The student body was on winter break, but the 1,179 people who entered the building that night would finally know the one thing I tried so desperately to hide. I didn't want anyone on campus to know that my dad was a drug addict. And because he embarrassed me on campus, I vowed to hate him for the rest of my life.

CHAPTER 14

JUDGEMENT: CONFESSING

Roman was the last to know. Jordyn wasn't aware of my newly assigned label until she heard me speak to a group of adjudicated youth in Wilmington, Delaware. I told Taylor myself when she came to my hotel room to visit me in New York. And Jerome II, well, he practically lived out every moment in real time. I asked each of my children to share their thoughts. I asked them to give me a recount of their emotional states—give me the optics of everything from their vantage points. I asked them to be raw and unapologetic. Were they sad, afraid, upset, angry, nervous, confused, numb and or shocked? I asked them to tell me if they were disappointed. I didn't quite yet ask for their forgiveness, though. But I was trying to gain some insight. In asking, I wanted to make sure they were aware that I knew, because of our interdependency, their lives would be changed forever.

I was their dad. They saw me as imperfectly perfect. They only had issues with my character when they didn't get their way. They were spoiled, privileged, and entitled. And I played a huge role in their current dispositions. Their childhoods were completely different from mine. I made sure of it. I tried to give with the right dose of appropriation. I never completely withheld. All four are good kids: respectable, solid students and model citizens. They've never done anything foreign, in terms of what normal kids do. And as a result, as parents, we tried to give according to our socio-economical abilities. But their forthcoming attitudes, when shocked by the word no, sometimes resembled that of ungratefulness.

I think most of it is forced to the forefront of our parental thoughts because we constantly walked around clutching the scars of an absentee father. I gave sometimes in excess because I never received. I gave, while kicking and screaming, because I desired to be taken care of as a child. I gave because I was their dad, and that's what dads are supposed to do. So when I did say no, it would be so damning to their souls that it forced them to immediately calculate how many times I said no to their siblings. And in turn, that manufactured a "favorite list." The reality of it all though is that they are all my favorites. They call me their "Old Head." And I call them my blessings from GOD.

There was no way of getting around telling Roman. Stories were released prior, but by the summer leading into the start of his fourth-grade school year, I ran out of time. I would finally have to talk to him about the entire ordeal. I kept wondering if it was possible to delay this conversation until he was much older. He was a typical 9-year-old, in Philadelphia for the summer, going to day camp at Abington Friends School and training at the Happy Hollow Recreation Center. Archery, swimming, basketball, Wawa's, Rita's Water Ice, and cheesesteaks— that was his childhood summer. After the Fourth of July holiday, Aida brought him and Jordyn to Las Vegas for the 2019 NBA Summer League. But outside of those nine days of competition, I didn't see

Roman at all that summer. He was having too much fun. My whereabouts was the last thing on his mind.

I was worried, however. I knew the kids would be back in Boston by late August. They usually returned to Boston two weeks before the start of school. From the end of the NBA Summer League until the day of their return, the only thing I could think about was my in-house attire. All the pajama pants I owned were made of thick flannel. It would be too hot for me to be walking around the house in pants, period. Especially flannel ones, at that.

As the day of Roman's return drew nearer, my stress intensified. I didn't want Roman to see the location monitor attached to my left ankle. I was sentenced to six months of home supervision and the anxiety of the awaiting conversation with a 9-year-old was causing me stress and nervousness. Roman is the child that kills me to my face, but to others he expresses the proudness of his affiliation. To others, it's always, my dad this and my dad that. But to my face, it's something different—you're old, bald and ugly. Deep down, though, he sees me as a grand figure. Now how am I gonna tell him the man he secretly idolizes went to jail, is a convicted felon, and as a result of my failure in character, has to report to a probation officer and can't move around freely? "If you want Chipotle for dinner Roman, I have to pick it up before 2:30 p.m." "Why so early, Dad?" "Because I can't leave the house after 3 p.m."

Tell me how that conversation is supposed to go. He's going to see the monitor. I'm not going to be able to hide it for six months. He's probably the most inquisitive of all of my children—not in a disrespectful way, but he's always asking questions. And he doesn't stop until he's either satisfied or threatened. "Roman, don't ask me again." "But

Dad, why?" "Ask me why one more time, and that's your ass." That's the only response that usually halts his line of questioning. I learned that from my mom. But I wasn't quite sure I would be able to get away with the threat this time. Roman had ammunition. He might hide his inquiry behind confusion. Or he might exercise sarcasm. "You broke the law, Dad? Oh, but you always tell me to tell the truth and to be honest and trustworthy. You even gave me a spanking for taking money out of Jordyn's room."

I was preparing myself for this response. At 9 years of age, Roman still needs guidance from a credible source. He's too young to be exposed to the chinks in his dad's armor. I was surprised that someone from his school hadn't discussed the current events of our family with their children, up until this point. I knew the entire community was following the story. Not because they were concerned for our family. But rather because they took pride in being an informed educational community. You sense the stares; you know they gossip. I even had a parent come up to me at a youth basketball game and tell me not to worry. As politely as I could, I said, "Do I look worried?" It wasn't her gesture that bothered me. It was the fact that I was reminded that I was carrying this weight. I was in a setting where I just wanted to be a crazy AAU parent, screaming at the refs, telling my son to shoot the ball. It was a Saturday morning, and this was my escape. I just wanted to be a dad. And quickly she reminded me of all the other shit that was going on in our lives.

I had it figured out. When Roman arrived, I was going to take him on a ride, just him and I, and confess. I already had confessed to my lawyer, to the government, to the FBI and to my employer. I owned it, held myself accountable and I didn't blame anyone, point fingers or make excuses. But confessing to a 9-year-old was by far the hardest conversation of them all.

CHAPTER 15

JUDGEMENT: STARBUCKS

Jordyn's response to my inquiry took place in the form of a letter. We were seated on the couch in our living room when I asked her to be raw and unapologetic. I wanted her to feel comfortable expressing those feelings to my face. After hearing my request, she paused. Two minutes later she told me she wasn't ready to talk about it. I told her I understood. What I didn't know was that her way of verbalizing the impact that my failure in character had on her would come in the form of an essay. She chose to write about it. She chose to share it with 15 college admission officers. Her college admission's Common App Essay explains how burden pushed her to purpose.

IN HER OWN WORDS

Walking into The Palestra's gala room, I tightened my grip on my oldest sister's hand. Cameras filled the Quaker themed event space, and their flashes blurred my vision when I joined my dad's side. At age 9, I had never liked being the center of attention. However, when my mom selected a gold-speckled dress and reminded my sister and I not to "act out," I knew I had to be on my A-Game for my family. My dad's induction into the Big Five Hall of Fame was one of the many celebrated moments I stood by his side, another accolade shelved on my list of reasons why I believed that he was invincible.

Eight years later, it's March, and my hands reach for my sister's grasp, but I resist the urge to expose my fear. Four concrete walls inside the Ferris Detention Center day room replaced the shiny walkway of The Palestra. The guards shuffled us in, and my dad, sister and I were escorted into a poorly furnished gymnasium space reserved for him to speak. We're surrounded by inmates and guards, and my dad, an invited guest, begins to share, "Hello! My name is Jerome Allen, and I'm one of the assistant coaches for the Boston Celtics." However, this time, instead of slipping in a prideful smile, he adds, "........and I'm a convicted felon." The room grows silent. My dad shares the grueling months of a mistake that led him to contemplate suicide, and his words are pieces of a story I had yet to hear.

Before the Center's revelation, mental health and my dad's case weren't topics our family directly discussed. During this period, I could not escape our family's over-whelming uncertainties. I struggled to motivate myself in school and crying myself to sleep became my new normal. I distanced myself from teachers and friends because I was terrified.

As JV soccer captain, Class of 2020 Co-President, and Varsity Basketball player, I learned to channel my energy elsewhere. I became an empathic listener, and I saw how my identity as a student-athlete, daughter, and sister, could potentially be impactful in spaces outside of my family's crisis. A year navigating different roles in school and at home showed me that nobody is perfect, and everyone experiences moments of self-doubt and lapses in judgement. The trip to Ferris forced me to reconcile my privilege. It also allowed me to witness pieces of my dad's past that I had never encountered. As I reflect on the kids of color at the Center and the stories they willingly shared with us, I couldn't help but consider how and why their life trajectories placed them behind bars. Many of the kids were my age and looked just like me. And yet I had the privilege of walking away afterwards. Being with them and hearing their stories shifted my perspective and purpose.

It wasn't until my dad's case that I realized how being a young woman of color impacts my ability to support and service people. There are still many uncertainties that I confront daily, but this past year has demonstrated that all people experience "messes" seemingly too difficult to escape. I have gained a level of self-awareness to tackle "messes" and uncertainties. And I know studying and advocating for social services and mental health will be mandated by my academic journey – regardless of where I'm accepted into college.

— Jordyn N. Allen, Dana Hall Class of 2020

Common App Essay

There were some things I held close to the chest. And if Jordyn hadn't been at Ferris Detention Center that day, I'm not sure she would have ever heard me verbally undress myself in that manner. I mean, I always talked to my kids about my general imperfections. But I stayed on the surface. I confessed to being a procrastinator and being moody. But I stood on the parental platform, gripping the ruling rod of "do as I say not as I do or did." So when asked if I ever smoked a cigarette, or if I ever consumed alcohol as a minor, I'd respond, "Yes." Only to normalize the temptation. Only in hopes that they realized I wasn't perfect. I broke rules and made mistakes and received punishment from my parents. I didn't get straight A's in school. I didn't always make my bed in the morning. And I picked fights with my sister and cousins.

I tried to take advantage of every teaching moment I could by sharing the appropriate stories at the appropriate times. I was their dad. I was larger than life in their eyes only because the imperfections I chose to share about myself didn't threaten my overall aura. Clark Kent can have blemishes while he's in plain clothes. But once he steps out of the phone booth, everything about him is perfect, including the neatly, slicked-back hair. As Superman, the world never observed the anxieties, the insecurities, the mental deficiencies that Clark Kent carried. Throughout my joust with The Alphabet, none of the kids, Jordyn included, ever saw my posture resemble anything less than invincible. But when alone, when not in costume, when at home in sweats, and not in smoothly pressed Italian suits, I suffered from a severe bout of depression. The guilt I carried washed away every ounce of faith I thought I had. If you would have asked me before my failure in character was announced to the world, I would have said, "Nothing can make me doubt God. Nothing." But feeling and living the consequences of my actions suppressed my physical state to the point where I contemplated suicide. Jordyn heard me tell the group of adjudicated youth seated in the common room at Ferris Detention Center the story about the day I almost took my own life.

This wasn't my first visit to Ferris. This wasn't a community service ploy. I knew that being an NBA assistant coach could grant me access to spaces I couldn't normally visit. The statistics state that one in four black males will have interaction with our nation's prison institution. The systemic and covert policies of our justice system have always charged me to extend a touch to those housed in these facilities. Long before receiving the convicted felon stamp, I visited Graterford State Correctional Institution's "Real Street Talk" program. I used to take Terry Rozier and Marcus Smart to visit the Department of Youth Services (DYS) Metro Regional Office in Dorchester, Massachusetts. And every time the Celtics traveled to Philadelphia to play the Sixers, I always connected with Elizabeth Cole so that I could go visit Ferris.

On this visit, my story, my dialogue, would resonate a little more with the population because I too was now in "the system." I wasn't delivering an empty message. I could relate to being handcuffed, being put in a holding cell, and being transported to court in shackles. They were excited. They wanted to hear about the Celtics and our star players.

But after I announced I was a convicted felon, they sat on every word that came out of my mouth. Maybe they were in disbelief, maybe it gave them hope—whatever it was that administered the paralysis, it allowed me to own the room. Some of the attendees in the common room remembered me from a previous visit. They remembered the BC Jerome—before conviction. I was back, and this time I had skin in the game. I never looked back at my two daughters to see the expression on their faces. I kept my eyes on the 45 adjudicated youth sitting inside the Ferris Detention Center's common room.

During the question and answer segment of my visit, one of the teenagers asked how I turned it around. He wanted to know what made me not go through with the attempt on my life. He asked what made me start trusting God again. I was floored by his questions. Most of the questions pertained strictly to basketball. Several elected to raise their hands to offer comments. They were just dying to articulate their allegiance to other NBA teams. The back and forth ribbing possessed a sensation that kept the room laughing. But the "trusting God again" question captivated the entire space. I told the group that regardless of their current positions and circumstances, their platforms still possessed enough power to make a difference in someone else's life.

I didn't want to use big words or talk over their heads. This was a population made up of court-committed youth from gang-infested neighborhoods throughout the state of Delaware. Some of its population even touched parts of Philadelphia and Delaware County. I wanted to meet them where they were at. It was important to me that, by the time I left, the group knew their lives had significance. I connected their significance to the "trusting God again" question. I told them another story. I even gave it a title and everything. It was called, "Do You Want Something to Drink?"

On the morning of Dec. 16, 2017, I woke up inside my hotel room in Memphis, Tennessee, and decided to walk to Starbucks. I could have gotten a free cup of coffee from the team's breakfast room inside the Westin Hotel, but I needed to get some fresh air. On previous trips to Memphis, I've taken the half-mile walk from The Westin Hotel to The Lorraine Motel, just to stand in the presence of significance. But this morning I decided to stroll to the Starbucks located right off the corner of the famous Beale Street.

Dressed in Celtics sweats from head to toe, I took a left out of the hotel, and then another left in front of the FedEx Forum. As I approached the Starbucks, I noticed a homeless man hovering over a small duffle bag. His other bag was used to support his rear end. He was an African American male, probably in his mid-30s. He didn't have a solicitation sign, nor did he whisper an ask as people walked by. He was just there. We locked eyes and I asked him if he wanted something to drink? He responded, "Anything hot. But what I really need is… I'm trying to come up with six dollars. It will afford me one night in the shelter…...until 6 a.m. But anything hot will be OK."

I walked inside Starbucks and ordered a grande cappuccino, a breakfast sandwich, and his hot tea. I told the barista to make whatever kind of tea was her favorite. The gentleman standing behind me in line asked if the tea was for the guy outside. I said, "Yes." Then he gestured to give me a dollar toward the cost of the tea. I said, "It's cool, I got it." The barista asked if I wanted honey, and then she informed me packets of sugar in the raw were located on the other side of the store. I grabbed the sugar and walked out of Starbucks.

As I walked back toward the homeless man, I noticed he had some dollar bills in his box. I instantly started to question the validity of his initial six-dollar request. I walked past him with this preconceived notion that he was a drunk or a drug addict. So when I saw the money in the box, I thought he was full of crap. I said to him, "Oh, I see your hustle."

He said, "It's four dollars." I barely looked at him. I handed him the tea and the breakfast sandwich and began to walk off. With both hands full, he glanced down at the second item and began expressing thankfulness. It was not unusual to witness someone's appreciation after an exchange, but this reaction caught me off guard. Probably because I thought he was secretly misleading the public. But his reaction to the unexpected sandwich that accompanied the tea really touched me. It was as if he really did want two items, but he'd simplified his request so he wouldn't appear to be obnoxious or ungrateful. I then reached in my pocket and said, "Hun, here's six dollars, also."

What he proceeded to say afterward not only changed my life, it saved my life.

He said, "Hey, you gotta have faith—pray and have faith."

I walked out of Starbucks to service a need. The beggar, the drunk, the addict, was in need of a kind gesture. In my judgement of his circumstances, I never would have expected him to know that I'd lost faith in God. How did he know I was angry, confused, sad, guilt-ridden, and depressed? How did he know The Alphabet issued their indictment and I could face imprisonment of up to 40 years? How did he know I planned to shoot myself in the head when the team got back to Boston? How did he know?

I went on to tell the group at Ferris that God speaks to us in many ways, and through many people. I told them you can't ignore or discredit the power of someone's platform. A homeless man saved my life. He shifted my perspective and consequently, I reclaimed my faith. I thought I was servicing him. But he ended up servicing me. When the team plane landed back in Boston, I threw the gun in the Charles River before I pulled into the parking garage of my apartment building.

CHAPTER 16
JUDGEMENT: MATTHEW 7:1

"Do not judge, or you too will be judged."

I lied earlier. Well, I'll say, I wasn't completely honest. I love all my children, love them all the same. There is nothing I wouldn't do for any of them. Since the first one came into this world at 3:05 p.m. Sept. 22, 1995, I've had a greater purpose in life. And to be blessed with four of them is something I'm truly grateful for. They all pull at my heartstrings. They all give me reason to get up in the morning. I would truly lay down my life for any of them. The downside to having multiple children is that their own optics can be skewed at times. They evaluate parental relationships with a certain bias that they refuse to admit, and they all possess triggers and internal drivers that feed their confirmative thoughts.

I had a board meeting on the same day and at the same time of Taylor's field hockey match and missed her first goal of the season. The next day, we held practice at 6:30 a.m., therefore my afternoon was free. So I showed up at my son's soccer match and instantly, Taylor records that in her validation radar as proof that Jerome II is my favorite. No thought or consideration as to my inability to get out of work responsibilities—just simply, "Oh. if his favorite has a game, he'll make time." It's crazy. And I try not to get stretched out, or too overwhelmed by the notion. But it does highlight one thing: and that is, children will fight their own siblings for the love and attention of a parent. The societal stigmas that come with being the youngest child, or the middle child, can and will be psychologically adopted by siblings from large families.

As parents our job is to love, nurture, provide, protect, and prepare—we are charged with producing participating citizens of the world. Each child may require a different focus, or different service from us, but we are still required to give exhausting effort. To invest in each child. So to have four children, with four different personalities, and four different sets of interests, can be quite stretching to any parent's composition. I don't rank them, although, some were easier to parent than others. I don't place any of them above the other. Again, I'd lay down my life for any of them.

But there has always been something about Taylor. Emotionally, I'm more sympathetic toward her. I give in at a much easier rate. She's the oldest girl, but the youngest twin. She came into the world two minutes after her brother. She's sensitive, she's the drama queen—and she's the toughest. Not to say the other three are soft. But after witnessing her go through four surgeries in high school, and still manage to play three varsity sports— let alone the six additional surgeries in college, while being president of her sorority chapter, I can't help but to have a special place for her inside my heart.

I mean, there were days she struggled against the malformation in her leg. We thought she would lose the leg to amputation at the age of six. But Taylor kept fighting. She was diagnosed with AVM—properly known as arteriovenous malformation. To this day, she's had 12 sur-geries. That's right, twelve. The first surgery was performed at Boston Children's Hospital, and the most recent one was done at Johns Hopkins in Baltimore, Maryland. The malformation has forced her to track down specialists all over the country. There were mornings her mom or her twin brother had to help her out of the bed. She would cry, but she wouldn't complain. She just managed the pain and found the strength to tough it out until the circulation allowed her to stroll with the slightest limp. She entered college desiring to be an English major. She applied to the College of Arts and Sciences at the University of Pennsylvania. But as her body physically matured, the malformation matured as well. It grew to cover her entire left thigh. And because of this constant health battle, she chose to transfer from the College of Arts and Sciences into the School of Nursing.

It pushed her to a new-found purpose. The inner school trans-fer put her an entire semester behind her original incoming class; the prerequisites she took the fall of her freshman year weren't needed in the School of Nursing. She would go on to pledge Alpha Kappa Alpha Sorority Inc., and eventually become President of the Gamma Epsilon Chapter. She ran for national office. She administered countless com-munity service projects and would eventually elect to do her Nursing Clinicals in Africa.

Taylor did her rotational clinicals at the Botswana Family Welfare Association (BOFWA) in Gaborone, Botswana. BOFWA is a sexual and reproductive health clinic that services underserved popula-tions—populations such as the LGBTQ community and sex workers. In Botswana, same-sex sexual acts just became legal in June 2019. So imagine the type of climate she worked in during the summer of 2018.

She told me one day they went to a maternity ward and newly crowned mothers were spread across the floor on mats holding their infants. The ward was just one open space with 24 mats placed on top of dust-covered floors.

It's safe to say, she was saddened by the conditions. In reflection, she realized how fortunate we were in the United States. She said the worst conditions possible didn't stop those people from smiling. She's crying and they are smiling. I saw her tears. We were on FaceTime and the only thing she kept saying was, "Dad, they seem so happy." Here she is falling apart because of their lack of resources. And simultaneously, they were smiling and being appreciative for what they did have. Prior to the two-day, sixteen-hour journey, she felt prepared. Penn's Nursing Program was ranked the No. 1 undergraduate nursing program in the country.

She felt like the University and all her professors equipped her with the right amount of knowledge, and the right amount of social and emotional capital to go and service this community. But no University could have prepared her for what laid ahead. The people she met and the places she was exposed to left such a lasting impression. She vowed to hold on to the lessons she learned, in hopes to be able to pass them on to those she'll be blessed to meet in the future.

She went to Botswana with the intention to teach, help and guide. Not only was she able to accomplish those things, but she also grew as a student and as a person. Someone from the clinic thanked her for coming. They stated to her that most of the nursing students that come from America don't look like the body that's being serviced. They thanked her for being a Black Woman, a Black American who cared. Taylor left Botswana so full, so excited, so ready to impact the world. Imagine returning to the States after such an experience and have to deal with one of the biggest headlines in American sports. The whole world just found out your dad pled guilty to a felony. Where do you go to hide?

The whispers, the stares, the awkwardness—she spent her entire life masking a stroll to avoid having people stare because of her limp. She refused handicap privileges that accompanied her disability. She would rather suffer the internal pain, grit her teeth, and frown her face, all for the appearance of walking normal. She didn't want people feeling sorry for her. Now, all that she hates, along with its uncomfort- ableness, is thrust upon her, because of her father's failure in character. Not because the AVM grew to be unbearable. But rather, because of her dad's reckless decisions.

Where do you go to hide when you don't want to deal with it at all? One more semester left until degree completion, she's forced to go back to campus and live in a dorm once occupied by her dad, some 24 years prior. Her fellow classmates, whom she befriended collectively her freshman year, aren't there to support her. They left campus imme- diately following graduation. And on top of that, her best friend just moved to Cape Town, South Africa. Now how do you think she can avoid being sad, depressed, angry, and bitter? She didn't ask for any of this attention. She just wanted to be a normal Penn nursing student. Yet, she was the daughter of the former coach who just got convicted of a felony. The whispers, the stares, the awkwardness, the loud silence— how could you not hate the person responsible for all of this social and emotional trauma?

You're living on campus, the same campus that represents the genesis of the infraction. You're trying to finish your last semester, trying to maintain your 3.3 GPA. But the school newspaper, the local newspapers, Twitter, Facebook and Instagram all keep running cycles of the story. Once she got over the shock of a potential 40-year sentencing from the original six charges on the indictment, her anger started to set in. "Why dad? Why?" Tears and loneliness. Have you ever been in a crowded space but felt lonely? At Penn, 9,999 under-graduate students march up and down the main artery of campus every day. There's one student though, the 10,000th, who chooses to walk outside the walls of the enclave because she's embarrassed. She needed to use Locust Walk more so than any other student. But the stares, the whispers, the awkwardness was too much. Forget about the AVM, forget about the limp, she'd rather cry from the pain of each step, each lunge, than cry from the unwanted attention.

BACHELOR OF SCIENCE IN ECONOMICS

WHARTON UNDERGRADUATE PROGRAM

GRADUATION CEREMONY

SUNDAY, MAY 13, 2018

UNIVERSITY OF PENNSYLVANIA

THE PALESTRA

KEYNOTE SPEAKER: JEFF WEINER W'92

CHIEF EXECUTIVE OFFICER, LINKEDIN

WHARTON DEAN: GEOFFREY GARRETT

In my six years as Head Coach at Penn, and my four years as a student athlete, I never entered an air-conditioned Palestra. Never. The lack of air added to the mystique of the building. In the winter the pipes talk to you; it's that old radiator heat at your grandmother's house. If the building is quiet enough you can hear the knocks and the hisses, as the heat circulates through the structure. The summers are different, however. No AC. I used to love working out in The Palestra during the summer. Even with the windows open, the air inside would be Philadelphia dry—that typical humid hot summer air. Those conditions are perfect when you're looking to gain sweat equity. Full-court defensive slide drills—two trips the length of the court performing that exercise will cause the perspiration lather to seep through your clothes.

I recall coaching a game against Harvard in early March one year. It was a sellout and The Palestra was rocking. The outside temperature that day peaked at 81 degrees, which was pretty unusual for that time of year. By tipoff, the temperature had dropped to 68 degrees, a perfect temperature for a pre-spring day. By the time our game reached overtime, I was out of a suit jacket and a tie. Both of my sleeves were rolled up past my elbows, and my armpits looked like I used water for deodorant. The 68-degree temperature, coupled with the 8,722 people in attendance, had The Palestra feeling "fish-grease hot." The building was rocking, and baking. As a player and as a coach, I don't remember all the wins. But I do remember all the losses—and I definitely remember that overtime loss. Not because of the blown "jump ball" call at the end of regulation, but more so because of how hot it was that night.

Special events will cause the University to artificially pump air into The Palestra. During President Obama's reelection campaign, a Democratic Party rally was held in The Palestra. Former President Bill Clinton was the speaker that evening. The back of The Palestra had giant slinkies covered with duct tape at one end, pumping frost condensation into the arena. I couldn't believe how cold this historical oven had gotten. I didn't attend the rally that evening, but I did walk inside the building hoping to get a glance of President Clinton in passing. I was inside long enough though to take note of the fact that the room temperature was being controlled by an outside tank—one that resembled the central air unit stationed outside of our home in Elkins Park. The only other time I was in an air-conditioned Palestra was for The Wharton School of Business Graduation Ceremony on May 13, 2018.

Each school at Penn holds its respective graduation ceremony separate from one another. And then all the schools combine to have one big commencement, which is always the Monday following Alumni Weekend. Of the four schools, Wharton houses the second largest number of students —1600, to be exact. So on the morning of the 13th, the air-conditioned Palestra was playing host to 400 Wharton graduates and their families. Even with all the lower bowl seats in use, it would be a struggle to squeeze 4,000 people into The Palestra. It was tight on this day, but they managed to get everyone inside. Roman, Jordyn and I barely made it, though. Our seats were high enough for us to use the wall as a back mount. That means we were on the last row.

When I heard his name called, I didn't clap, I didn't scream, I didn't even blurt out a loud YEAH! I just sat there. I was so paralyzed by the surreal-ness of it all that it forced me to be still. It made me be more in awe of God. I mean I heard all of his family, all of his friends, I even heard the windows slightly shaking. He did it. He didn't just graduate. He transformed the space we all called the University of Pennsylvania. He did it his way, and on his terms. For me to be in attendance in the same building where so many cheered me on as a player, and hear people cheer him on for reasons other than sports, gave me a feeling that surpasses the limitations associated with being a proud parent. I was beyond proud. He became my idol. And here's how he did it....

The day before the Wharton Graduation, the Office of the President of the University held the traditional Senior Honors Ceremony. "Ivy Day" Ceremony is held every Saturday of Alumni Weekend. This would be the 145th gathering of such a day. In recognition of outstanding leadership and service to the University community, students of the senior class, both male and female, receive symbolic ornaments that highlight their undergraduate contributions. These selected bodies cover the entire senior class, some 2500 students. Eight awards, total: four male student awards and four female student awards. There isn't any politics or campaigning going on; election is strictly determined by your fellow students. It's a true reflection of how your peers see you.

Four male awards correspond to the ranking in which your peers viewed your significance. The four awards go as follows: Spoon, Bowl, Cane and Spade—with the "Spoon" being the highest. Former United States congressman from the state of Tennessee, Harold Ford, won the Spoon in 1992. John Wideman, the Rhodes Scholar and only writer to win the PEN/ Faulkner Award for fiction two times, won the Spoon in 1963. Seth Berger, the founder of AND1, won the Bowl in 1989. The current chaplain of the University, Charles Howard, won the Bowl in 2000. Huntsman Hall, the home of the Wharton Business School, is named after the Spoon recipient from the class of 1959, John M. Huntsman. Needless to say, congressmen, philanthropists, chaplains— all are members of this distinguished group.

Jerome won the Bowl Award at the 2018 Ivy Day Ceremony. The impact he had on campus wasn't something he celebrated, blogged or tweeted about—he just went about. He went about having impact so silently that it almost seemed improbable. Nowadays everybody posts and tweets everything. It's become a social norm. But he went about things differently. He popped in and out of spaces and circles and consumed everything and touched everybody in such a genuine manner. He knew who he was, he embraced his story, and as a result, he had a tremendous impact on campus. I didn't know about half the things he did. I just kept saying, when did he have time to do it all? I mean, he ignored my phone calls sometimes, but that's what all children do to their parents when they go away to college. But to do all that he did on campus, and do it quietly? Man, that was impressive. It had to take deliberate effort and focus. I asked him how and why he locked in and serviced the campus the way he did?

And he simply said, "Because of you—I was tired of being referenced to as your son. I was tired of people coming up to me and asking me how you were doing before they even asked me how I was doing. I was tired of sharing space. I was in my mother's womb at the same time as my sister. We went to preschool, elementary school, middle school, high school and college together. I had the same name as you. So, every sports circle I walked into, people asked if I was as good as my dad. You wore #53, I purposely chose #35. You played basketball; my sport of choice was baseball. I just wanted to be me, for once in my life. I wanted to prove to everyone that I'm unique, that I was special. That I was Jerome, not your son, not the twin.

"I just wanted to make a difference, independent of my biological relationship. I begged you to let me take a gap year after graduation because I need to go somewhere by myself, where no one knows me. Where I have to figure stuff out on my own. Where I can be alone, so I can find myself. All my life I've shared space and a name. Once I got to Penn I was determined to have impact, I was determined to be me.

That's where I got the drive, why my effort and focus were deliberate. And Dad, guess what? I did it."

The day after the Ivy Day Ceremony, Wharton's graduation was held in the air-conditioned Palestra. Jerome won the Dean's Award for Service to Penn and the Philadelphia Community. Dean Garrett read off all that Jerome did, and the building erupted after hearing every entity he serviced. I just sat there, tears rolling down my eyes because he exhausted himself in his experience: President of Penn Club Baseball, Head RTA for Wharton's Sports Business Academy, RTA for Wharton's Leadership in the Business World, Co-Founder of Adolescent Father Initiative, TA for Management Recitations, proctor for Building Bridges to Wealth classes at Wharton, President of Black Men United, member of Black Wharton, interned at Morgan Stanley, and was a Co-Founder of the Wharton Sports Business Summit. And he graduated with a dual concentration in Strategic Management and Legal Studies.

Here's an example of the impact he had: On Dec. 4, 2019, "Market Insiders" wrote an article highlighting Wharton's new Sports Analytics and Business Initiative (WSABI). This initiative sprung to life immediately following the school's acceptance of a $15,000,000 anonymous gift. Coincidently, The Wharton Sports Business Summit had just completed its third iteration. Now in my opinion, Wharton established this new initiative in sports because of the efforts of undergrad student-led groups and organizations. The leaders of those organizations not only had a passion for sports but saw the opportunities on the business side that typical Wharton overseers were ignoring. The Summit was an event that various student groups, MBA groups and alumni, could use as a platform to share the work they are doing in sports. Jerome and the other two co-founders used the Summit as a means to connect alumni back to Penn. After its third installment, more media coverage, more "big name" alumni involvement, and 3 straight years of selling out, there has been an influx of capital to support student led groups on campus.

Jerome and Jared, one of the other Summit Co-Founders, who started the analytics and research group, led the Undergraduate Sports Business Club their junior and senior year. They both saw that Wharton wasn't doing enough with sports. Every Wharton student was running down the typical path to finance or consulting. So when they brought up the idea of organizing the summit, they were discouraged by faculty. Probably because other undergrad groups, MBA students, and Law School students had tried to put on similar events in the past and flopped. Their task was to not only to put on a great event, but to facilitate something that would last years into the future.

What they didn't anticipate was multimillion-dollar investments into Everything Sports at Wharton. The Summit helped Penn/Wharton generate revenue streams, create research opportunities, and pilot interdisciplinary studies. It blows my mind that the nation's No. 1 business school doesn't have a sports specific degree at the undergraduate or MBA level. The valuation of sports franchises is growing faster than 60% of the commodities on the stock market. There are a ton of drivers that can be attributed to this occurrence. Penn and Wharton possess a unique position at the center of value creation and comprehension in sports. Jerome gives all the credit for his recognition and awareness to his Wharton faculty mentors Kenneth Shropshire, Scott Rosner and Keith Weigelt.

Him and I have this debate all the time about success vs significance. His significance will go unnoticed by many. But in my opinion, he left Penn better than he found it. Future opportunities will open up for undergrads, and many will have him to thank for it. He won the Dean's Award for Service to Penn and the Philadelphia Community at the Class of 2018 Wharton Graduation. And he won the Bowl at the Class of 2018 Ivy Day Ceremony. He walked into Penn as the oldest child of the Men's Basketball Coach at Penn. He left Penn as his own entity. Jerome B. Allen II—my idol.

If you type "Jerome Allen +University of Pennsylvania" into a search engine, every article that was written about my indictment, guilty plea, and sentencing pops up. Every single one. Nothing surfaces that hints at, or supportively suggests distinction. There are thousands of characters named Jerome Allen in this country. But there are only two individuals that go by that name and bear a connection to the University of Pennsylvania. My failure is not only fresh, it's so significant that historical drippings will always leave residue around the school, its athletic department and my identity.

Never will the first mention of Jerome Allen and the University deliver results that raise the question which one? The former coach of the men's basketball team? The former coach who is a convicted felon now? Or the 2018 Wharton grad who won the Dean's Award and the Bowl? Never will the search engine make the distinction. For a young man to work so hard to create his own path, and yet still be forced to attach himself to something he had absolutely nothing to do with, is unfair.

It's sad. Guilty by association because of his namesake. How would you feel if you received unwanted stares, if you were administered employment rejections, if your character was questioned because of someone else's failure in character? You'd be pissed, angry, sad, depressed, lonely, and bitter. My dad's failure in character was witnessed by 1,179 fans in attendance at The Palestra. Twenty-four years later, my failure in character was witnessed by the entire world.

I went to my dorm after he embarrassed me. My son went halfway across the world after I embarrassed him. At first, I thought that he would never come back from South Africa. I thought he would just stay there and live his life. I wouldn't blame him at all. I deserved to lose him. But as much as I tried to hide behind the self-imposed guilt, I was crying, hoping he would forgive me. I tried so desperately to help the community, to help other young men, and here I was not servicing my own child.

He lashed out and condemned me for the hypocrisy in my life. He gave me his unapologetic truth. The words were hard to hear, but necessary. My idol wasn't willing to just say," It's OK dad, people make mistakes, I love you and I forgive you." No compassion, no sympathy, no forgiveness—nothing. Just hate. The same hate I vowed to have towards my dad for the rest of my life. The two infractions don't even compare. My dad was sick with an addiction. I, on the other hand, was arrogant and reckless, with disregard to positions and processes.

God has a funny way of exposing us to the inconsistencies in our own lives. When the judge gets judged. When we judge, we ignore perspective, we disregard content. Because our process, in terms of evaluating action, won't allow us to fully grasp the Why associated with a decision—we tend to simply judge. Situational or personal attributes may render a Why in conjunction with the occurrence. However, human beings' defaults will always land on judgement. We never choose to allow patience and perspective to reign. We don't pause to peel back the layers. Rarely will we address thought and its cognitive function. But when the shoe is on the other foot, somehow we hope the entity doing the evaluation has understanding, empathy, compassion and or grace to offer. It took 45 years for God to expose the hypocrisy I was carrying. I carried it like I carried my wallet. It went everywhere with me—driver's license, insurance card, credit card and hypocrisy.

Each of the kids were greatly affected by my failure in character. Just like Jonah's disobedience impacted the sailors on the boat, my failure greatly affected their journeys as well. My dad's episode at The Palestra was merely that, just an episode. My life, my sense of normalcy wasn't altered. And yet I wanted him erased from my life. What I did to my own kids could have had catastrophic consequences. One could argue that the trauma from the occurrences will be carried by each one for the rest of their lives. I'm thankful, though, for the exposure of both the infraction and the hypocrisy. For without the exposure of the infraction, I'd never get to address the hypocrisy.

PART III

The ultimate measure of a man is not where he stands in moments of comfort and convenience, but where he stands at times of challenge and controversy.

DR. MARTIN LUTHER KING, JR.

CHAPTER 17

PREJUDICE

We are all prejudiced. All of us prejudge our experiences when we are in the moment. The value we place on such is significant. It's computed based on the tags assigned by our eyes, and the sensations they carry emotionally. However, that value ignores perspective. When we reflect on those same experiences, we tend to place a different value on that which has transpired. Upon reflection, the present value of the experience is always less than, or greater than the quantitative summation of the reflection. Here's what I mean.

One day I asked my boss if I could leave the job site early. He entertained my request, and then politely said, "No." I lost it. I started calling him all types of names—under my breath, though. I instantly allowed his response, his denial, to affect my entire attitude. For the next two hours on the job, I wasn't effective or efficient. My value contribution radar was significantly low. All because the supervisor would not let me leave earlier than my contract stated. I wanted to be compensated even in absence. My sense of entitlement forced a shift in perspective: "Man, I hate him. I'm about to give him my two weeks' notice." One hundred twenty minutes passed, and I ran to my car. I didn't say goodnight to anyone in the department. Face still frowned up, posture still tensed, wearing all my emotions on my sleeve—my entire essence was saying, "Fuck you and this job." I pressed the elevator button, not with my index finger, but with the mountainous bump of a balled-up fist. Down the elevator, to the garage, walking knock-kneed, hard. Not as hard as Spike Lee in "Do the Right Thing," but close enough. I hit the alarm, opened the car door, flopped down in the drivers' seat, and slammed the door shut. Now how dumb is that? Abusing my own car all because he wouldn't let me go home early.

Once I cleared the employee parking garage, I turned on my favorite local radio station. Doc B was in the middle of a 5 o'clock traffic jam mix. It was the midpoint of the mix and typically the only interruption during this commercial-free period is for a traffic update. A young lady's voice rose above the lowered volume of the mix and she began to report, "Traffic still backed up on I-76 West. There was an earlier accident at the 30th Street on-ramp. Ten cars were involved; 4 are dead, 9 others injured. If you're traveling on I-76 you're advised to avoid this area, as it's been a log jam since the collision happened at 3:30 this afternoon."

At first, when I heard her say 3:30, I didn't think anything of it. Her voice continued to sadden, not because of the normalization of car accidents, but rather, because two of the four who were pronounced dead at the scene were children ages nine and 13. I too followed the sentiment in her voice. Then I thought, wait a minute, I would have been entering I-76 from that on-ramp at the same exact time, if my supervisor had granted my request to leave early. Instantly, I changed my attitude and self-conversation. I started saying, "Thank God he didn't let me leave early, because I would have been right in the middle of that pileup."

At the moment of rejection, I thought his response was the worst thing ever! I was ready to pivot to emptiness—all because of a no. Now I'm thanking him because his response allowed me to avoid something that could have been catastrophic. You see, events in real time always have a different valuation upon reflection. So thank God for your no's sometimes. We don't even know about half of the things He's protected us from.

In 2014, I thought I was one year away from being able to sustain success at Penn. However, everybody knows a losing record, plus a new athletic director, equals firing. In the back of my mind, I always knew this was a possibility. So going into the 2014-15 season, I convinced myself that the best way to approach the upcoming season, the recruits, the team, the University and the alumni, was to act as if I was on a lifetime contract. Sell the school, the Ivy brand, and the program.

It's an easy sell for someone whose life trajectory was generationally altered by the product itself. I graduated from the University. I had a set of twins who were set to begin their freshman year at the University. My wife was a student in the Liberal Arts and Professional Studies Program. And for the past 19 years, my children, my mother, my sister, my niece, and my cousins all claimed the Quakers as their favorite college basketball team. We were (and still are, for the record) Quakers. We loved the school. I'm Wharton '09, Jerome II is Wharton '18, Taylor is Nursing '18, and Smoke, Terry, Freddie, Shank, Darnell, Main-e-Ack and Goodah, are all UPenn Class of '95.

Understand, when I left 4601 Germantown Ave., all my cousins and friends from the Ave left with me. Nineteen minutes by car, one hour five minutes by public transportation—7 miles separated my grandparents' house and the W.E.B. DuBois College House on UPenn's campus. The 23 trolley to the Broad Street Subway, and then Broad Street Subway to the Market-Frankfort L Train—that route transported the eight of us to an enclave of peace that none of us could have foreseen.

We either slept in my dorm room or in The Palestra. Where we slept was usually determined by my actual roommates' tolerance level for that particular evening. Sometimes we even slept in Weightman Hall. Overcrowded crack houses in the summertime didn't have the same ventilation or space as Weightman Hall had to offer. I remember Smoke, Terry, Shank, and I were hanging out late one Friday night. Instead of disturbing my three assigned roommates' peace and quiet, we decided to go sleep in The Palestra for the night. Smoke and Man Man found rest on top of the two training tables inside our team locker room. And Shank and I were stretched out on the floor. No pillows, or blankets. Just us—we supported and covered one another. When we woke up Saturday late morning, St. Bonaventure was about to play Rhode Island in the first round of the Atlantic 10 Conference Tournament. The four of us just started laughing.

By my sophomore year, my family was around the dorm so much that the security guards didn't make my presence or signature a requirement for them to enter. I'd come home from a road game and it was normal to see Freddie asleep on the lobby couch. They became such staples on campus that even other students who lived on my dorm floor let my family crash in their rooms. All of us went to Penn together. We shared space in my room, and we shared meals from the dining hall. The only thing we didn't share though, was my classroom responsibilities. That was all on me. But at least they made sure I was awake in time for my 8 a.m. Calculus Recitation. Well, sometimes.

By the end of the 2014-15 season, with a combined record of 65-104, it's fair to say forced resignation was the only option I should have been afforded. Since 1948, UPenn has had 10 coaches lead the men's basketball program. I was the only coach over my tenure never to win an Ivy League Championship. Nine out of ten head coaches had been successful in obtaining at least one, but not I. So I understood. I got it. The new athletic director, in her first year at UPenn, made a statement. Men's Basketball is the flagship sport at the University, and it was in desperate need of a change in leadership. It didn't matter that I felt like we were right there, ready to turn the corner. It didn't matter that I once wore the red and blue uniform. It didn't matter that I helped develop the program's last Ivy League Player of the Year. It didn't matter that my family loved the University. We weren't winning and that wasn't acceptable.

On Monday, March 2, 2015, I agreed to step down as the John R. Rockwell Head Coach of Men's Basketball at the University of Pennsylvania. I wanted to beg for one more year. I felt like I let the University and its 300,000 alumni down. I felt like I didn't leave it better than I found it. I felt like I failed. So going into my last Ivy weekend, with three games remaining in our season, I kept my firing (or forced resignation, however you want to put it) a secret. I only told the coaching staff. We were co-workers, we were a family. I wanted them to digest the news, but also understand why it was important that we continue to coach hard throughout the remaining games. We owed it to the University, more importantly, we owed it to our players.

All week we prepared our guys for the Columbia/Cornell, Friday/ Saturday back-to-back home stand, as if I had that lifetime contract. Earlier in the week, we tried to expose the team to concepts they could possibly see on both nights. As we got closer to Friday's game, we tended to narrow the focus toward Friday nights' opponent. With such a quick turnaround, we treated Saturday's shootaround more like a walkthrough. No tape, non-contact, light jog, is what we required of the team. One o'clock film, 1:30 p.m. walkthrough, 3 p.m. team meal—for six years as a coach and four years as a player that was our Ivy back-to-back Saturday schedule. Film and walkthrough times could flip-flop, depending upon whether it was the second game against a league opponent. This shootaround, I decided to do a walkthrough before we showed the film.

As the team stretched in the middle of the court, I was informed by one of the assistant coaches that the ESPN ticker was reporting I would not return next year as UPenn's coach. I instantly broke out into a sweat. What was I going to do? My mind started racing. My anxiety went to 100 real quick. I'm trying to make sure we cover the defensive points of emphasis for the upcoming game, but now there's an elephant in the room. What was more important—the guys having an understanding of Cornell's desired outcomes? Or making sure they were ready to compete with a clear mind? What could hinder them from having a clear mind? I'm sweating and stumbling over my words, because I hadn't told the players that I'd stepped down (been fired). And the last thing I wanted was for them not to hear it from me first. I'd been around college and professional sports long enough to know that the first thing players do when they walk off the court is grab their cell phones.

My firing was on the bottom ticker of ESPN and everyone connected to college basketball, both directly and indirectly, would now know information that only my staff and the other two individuals who were present in that Monday meeting knew. As we got deeper into the Cornell scout, I somehow managed to grasp enough calmness to inform the players that they were not allowed to look at their phones post-shootaround until I walked into the locker room. Nothing all week. Who knows who leaked the info. Everyone was holding onto plausible deniability. I must be honest though; the leak shifted my understanding. I was starting to become bitter. I lost perspective.

CHAPTER 18

TIMING AND METHOD

As the pressure from the FBI and the United States Attorney's Office continued to mount during the beginning of 2018, I kept thinking about the enormity the case would potentially have had if I were still coaching at UPenn at the time of exposure. If my failures in character had been exposed while still employed by the University, I would have been thrown under the jail right away. Literally. There was a huge college basketball scandal transpiring, and my case was adjacently leaning against it. Mine, however, lent a different commentary. It was almost a reverse scenario, in terms of the exchange. At the time of exposure, being removed from the genesis of the infraction afforded me a couple of things, time being one. I had time to reflect on the AD's decision in March 2015. I also had time to secure other employment. And time to build relationships in that setting.

In reflection, I'm now thankful the AD went with a change in leadership. It allowed me to fall underneath a leadership group that addressed my failure in character without the punitive condemnation some may have thought it required. They allowed me to take ownership of the self-created storm. So I'm glad the exposure happened when it did—while I was an assistant coach for the Boston Celtics. It happened when I was connected to the biggest platform this sport has to offer. And although the range of media coverage at the professional level dwarfs the collegiate level, it was best that it happened then. Every media outlet wrote about it—Bloomberg News, Sports Illustrated, ESPN, The Philadelphia Daily News, The Philadelphia Inquirer, Philly.com, Bleacher Report, The Wall Street Journal—and I'm sure I'm forgetting some. Upon reflection though, I can boldly say, trust God for the timing and method of your exposure.

The greatest time for God to use you could be when things are at their worst. The prejudice value I placed on all that had transpired became different. Quietly, I almost lost my mind. But if I'm reflecting on it that means I got through it. I charged myself guilty. I hold myself accountable. I blame no one. I had a failure in character. I kept thinking about the Disciple Peter and his outing in the courtyard. The location and timing didn't forfeit an opportunity for God to still use him. Now, I would never compare the significance of my exposure to the man responsible for starting the modern-day Christian Church. And as much as I prayed to God asking Him to speak to my crisis, I would be remiss if I didn't acknowledge what God has shown me—and that was, despite my imperfections, despite my failure in character, the timing and location of everything will not affect His ability to still use me.

Your significance in failure can't be ignored. David, Peter and yes, you and I, all have failed at one point or another. Our integrity didn't match the platforms mankind afforded us. By no means am I comparing myself to biblical icons, but I am aware of the lessons their stories can teach us about the human elements in all of us. Those imperfections, which may lead us to failure at some point in time, do not, however, forfeit our purpose, our calling. In fact, I'd argue that our failures are necessary for us to get to the next season of our lives. It is in failure that we receive the necessary boost, the springboard, the proper purging that brings forth the ultimate service designed for others.

It sounds crazy to say that only exposure to burden, or exposure to failure, can bring us to purpose. Failure can force the required transparency of self, so that lives can be saved. I failed just like so many others have done in the past. It's my prayer that like the Disciple Peter, the timing and location of my failure does not forfeit the significance of my being. It amazes me that throughout the Bible, God chose broken individuals to move others forward. So again, I pray that the significance of my failure draws others to Christ.

CHAPTER 19

REPUTATION VS. INTEGRITY

On April 6, 2018, the FBI, several Assistant US Attorneys, and the IRS showed up at my lawyer's office. My first encounter with The Alphabet took place 436 days prior at TD Garden. Then, it was only two agents. However, this time, we met in a conference room at Harvard University Law School and they were eight-deep. Arresting officers, attorneys, forensic specialists—they brought the entire team. I wasn't expecting this type of greeting. But so much had transpired between the first encounter and now that I wasn't surprised by the size of the group. It was intimidating, but not totally overwhelming. Ron had prepared me for the worse, but as much forward thinking we had done to prepare, I still was nervous. Being pierced by 16 eyeballs would make anyone uneasy. Every word analyzed, every movement in posture, studied. It's like coming home after a night out with the fellas and as soon as you hit the door your spouse is standing there, arms folded across their chest, studying your speech patterns.

Uncomfortable is an understatement. I prayed and prayed and prayed that this day could be avoided. The anxiety attached to waiting does more damage to the spirit than the actual occurrence of that which you are waiting for. The Alphabet had come, and was continuing to come, whether I wanted them to or not. I was hoping my will and God's will were in alignment, though. But once the April 6 date was established, I couldn't help but think this could possibly be my arrest day. How fitting, on the campus of probably the best university in the world I'd be taken away for a crime I committed on another university's campus.

My lawyer, the great Morehouse Man he was, the great husband and father he was, was also a phenomenal Harvard Law School professor. He provided that sense of comfort you get when you go get your big brother to defend you against the neighborhood bully. Originally, I didn't want to call him. I knew I needed representation, but I didn't want to solicit anyone who knew me personally. Ron's son and my youngest son were classmates at an independent school in Weston, Massachusetts. Being the only two boys of color in their entire class meant it was our responsibility as parents, to make sure our young black boys had a true sense of identity, from support to awareness. We were black fathers, we were active and engaged — fall concerts, science fairs, parent/ teacher coffees. Neither he nor I would ever have imagined that one day he'd be my final frontier of defense, the human shield covering me from the custodial time awaiting on the horizon.

I didn't want to call him. I was too embarrassed. Not one of the parents from my son's class. I was scarred by the stigmas that come with being the parent of private school kids: bad drivers, yoga pants and gossipers, always in other people's business. Aida insisted, however. And boy am I glad I listened to her. Maybe if I would have listened to her more throughout our marriage, I wouldn't be in this mess in the first place.

The morning started off like a typical morning anytime I'm home in Boston during the season. I woke up at 5:45 a.m., showered, got dressed, hugged Aida, jumped in the car, and then proceeded to navigate through the congested highways and streets of Metro Boston to drop the kids off at school. My timeline on the journey dictated the car's atmosphere. From the house to The Meadowbrook School, the dialogue normally centers on Roman's upcoming assignments, or NBA highlights or Old School versus New School music. Only Beyoncé's "Homecoming" made Roman appreciate Frankie Beverly. And only BET's airing of The New Edition Story gave "Candy Girl" and "If It Isn't Love" relevance in Roman's world. Once he exits the car, 25 minutes into the commute, Jordyn and I religiously listen to The Breakfast Club's nationally syndicated show. When we lived in Philadelphia, before we backed out of the driveway, the first thing the three of us did was turn on The Yolanda Adams Morning Show. The kids knew the rules: we had to listen to one song from the Christian genre before I let them control the car radio. Now that we were living in Boston, and Jordyn was much older, I felt like Angela Ye's "Rumor Report" or Charlamayne's "Donkey of the Day" wasn't too intense for her ears. Plus, she probably was gonna be exposed to the same "radio censored" information on social media anyway.

After Jordyn exits the car, I usually stop in the Dunkin' Donuts on Washington Street in Wellesley, Massachusetts, to grab a small hot coffee, with two creams and three sugars. Its slow intake is fitting for the minimal 50-minute drive from the Dana Hall School to the Boston Celtics' practice facility. I hate traffic. But this hour drive affords me alone time, quiet time, reflection time and or connecting time. However I chose to spend it, whether it is calling the twins or my mom, or listening to music, TED talks, podcasts, sermons and or silence, I almost always never stressed, or worried about anything during this time.

But April 6, 2018, after the kids got out of the car, everything became a blur. What if they take me into custody? I won't be able to pick them up from school. Do I call Pooh and Tee and give them a heads up? I promised Ro and Jo that they could go early to TD Garden with me today. They both loved going early to the arena. We had a 7:30 p.m. tip vs the Chicago Bulls, and Roman was anticipating shooting around before the players got on the floor. This was the highlight of his Fridays, not the all school early dismissal on Fridays. But rather, game day Fridays when he could go shoot around on the Garden floor.

Being stressed and calm at the same time is a weird feeling. I adopted the posture of not always appearing as though I was a victim. I was trying to accept uncertainty. More so, I was trying to be comfortable with being uncomfortable. It's hard. Plus, I didn't want to make my stress obvious to the world. In trying to mask it all, while you're carrying your hidden burdens, you get upset anytime someone either asks you for something or asks you to do something. That's exactly how I felt the day School Based Youth Services (SBYS) of Camden, New Jersey, asked if I would do the second iteration of the Adolescent Fathers Initiative. And they wanted it to be on the same day I had to meet with The Alphabet. I was like, "Lord, please, no. I don't want to deal with these kids. Not right now. Don't they know I'm fighting for my life? Lord, please, remove it all, remove this infraction, remove SBYS's request. I can't deal with it right now. I understand, Lord, and I get it — it's the only day that works for the District. But Lord, you know I got some other shit going on right now. I can't be setting up visits to Harvard on the same day. What if they take me into custody? That will be even worse. Please, not today, Lord."

My meeting with The Alphabet lasted three and a half hours. I knew the commute from Cambridge to Weston and then to Wellesley would take well over an hour at that time of day. But if I got stuck in traffic driving to pick the kids up, then that means I didn't get arrested. So I would be the happiest person on the road. No road rage for me. I'd be happy to drive across town, pick the kids up, and then drive back to Cambridge to meet the 16 high school students who took the coach bus from Camden. Not getting arrested meant I would have the chance to stand outside of Harvard's Kennedy School of Government to greet them.

At 10 a.m. I was in a suit and tie getting drilled by The Alphabet. By 2:45 p.m. that same day, I was back on campus attempting to use exposure and truth-telling to inspire and motivate a group of students who had previously never ventured out of the state of New Jersey. We were back on Harvard's campus putting on another seminar addressing identity, social norms, and thought. We were still attempting to leverage the stories and journeys of Harvard men. It was our attempt to instill belief in young men who were forced to navigate resource-challenged communities and educational spaces.

At the intersection of Massachusetts Avenue and John F. Kennedy Street, 16 students and four chaperones stood patiently waiting for my arrival. None of them knew what I had experienced one hour and 30 minutes earlier. They were excited and anxious. The only thing I saw as I turned the corner were smiles. They made it to Harvard. Forget the six hours and 30 minutes they sat on the bus. No complaining, no restlessness. The euphoria from their current location had them floating.

I, on the other hand, was an emotional wreck. The fluctuation, the nervousness, the sadness, the anxiety, the joy, the relief, the worrying, the anticipation, the thankfulness—by the time I exited Soldiers Field Road to meet the group, I thought I was gonna pass out. But, when I saw how excited the group was, I gained strength. My lens was starting to shift. None of this was about me.

Again, I prayed for the infraction to be removed. I prayed for the boys' trip to be canceled. But God had different plans. It was as if He told me, "Yeah, I hear you. I see your tears and I know you're sorry. But while you're asking me to service you, I got somebody I need you to service. Don't worry, I'm gonna get in your self- created storm and manage it. Not the way you want, though. But it will play out so that there will be no argument as to who should get the glory. In the meantime, take care of the boys. Show them that anything is possible. Take them to the Celtics/Bulls game tonight. Let them meet Marcus Morris and Terry Rozier. Let Jayson Tatum meet them for breakfast in the morning. Have him tell them his story about being a teenage dad. Let them go shopping. Share your sneaker collection with them. Give, invest, encourage. I'm well aware of what you have going on. Right now, though, I need you to focus on this group."

But when you're fighting for your life, it's hard to think of others first.

Two days before my 20th wedding anniversary, and four days before Bloomberg News broke the original story, I sat in the parking lot of King of Prussia Mall waiting for the Hermes store to open. I had picked out the perfect gift to commemorate this milestone. Twenty years is a long time—and I give her all the credit for holding us together. I still don't know how or why she's put up with me for all these years. Proverbs 18:22 states, "He who finds a wife finds what is good and receives favor from the Lord." It didn't take 20 years for me to believe this verse; however, because of my own brokenness, I was just becoming fully aware of the blessing I had.

I got to the parking lot at 9:45 a.m. The Las Vegas NBA Summer League had just wrapped up, so Aida and I decided to spend a couple of days in Philly before we took off for the NBA Cares/Basketball Without Borders event in Johannesburg, South Africa. Normally, post summer league, Coach Stevens encourages the staff to get out of the office and recharge our batteries. So being in Philly this time of the year wasn't particularly odd for me. Aida, Roman and myself were all anticipating the upcoming trip to Africa. It was a dream come true. I always wanted to go. Although I had no direct line in terms of exact lineage, I looked at the entire continent as being of significance to me.

My general ignorance could have been resolved by simply testing with Ancestry.com. But I've never truly been in search of the exact location of my ancestors. Our story in America has been so traumatic that honestly speaking, I claim the entire continent. At the time, Taylor was in Botswana doing her nursing clinicals, and Jerome was in Cape Town working in a township for the CT Ten Foundation. They had planned to meet us in Johannesburg. Jordyn would be the only one missing. She was doing a 7-week STEM and bio summer program at UPenn. I couldn't believe I was going to Africa and that I was going to be able to share the experience with my family.

I planned on using my debit card to make the purchase for Aida. My card had been copied twice so I was extremely cautious about where I used it and how much money it carried. Normally, if I knew I was going to make a significant purchase, I would transfer funds into the account right before the sale was executed. So, since I had a couple of minutes before the mall opened, I decided to pull out my phone and transfer the money while I sat in the car. I logged on to my Citizens Bank account, only to find all four of my accounts in the red. Each one had been levied. And this was icing on the cake, because five days before this parking lot relegation, I was hit with a six-figure tax lien by the IRS. So to keep from crying, I just started laughing. With a slight smirk on my face, I whispered to myself, "Lord what else?" I had $60 in my wallet. As a matter of fact, I had $60 to my name—nothing in a shoe box or under a mattress. I sat in the car, put my head down, and started beating on the steering wheel. As I tapped on the steering wheel, I said, "Man, The Alphabet don't play fair."

On July 20, 2018, Bloomberg News informed the world that I testified at a grand jury hearing. It sent shockwaves through every community I was associated with. I had a great reputation as a kind-hearted, loyal, upstanding, humble guy, who seems quiet and shy at times. One may interpret those qualities and automatically assume they belong to a man with integrity. Up until now I had worn the attributes of good character so well that those who knew me would swear my reputation and integrity matched. But my eventual guilty plea would prove that reputation and integrity are two different things.

4th Birthday with Dad, 1977

1973

1986, Logan PAL 12-14 Year-Old Age Division, City Champs REAR, (L) Officer Mel Kilgore; REAR, second from RIGHT, me.

Episcopal Academy Basketball Team, 1989-90. My junior year, #53.

My friends. Graduation Day, Woodrow Wilson Jr. High.

Fall, 1988. Undefeated season for the Philadelphia Little Quakers AAU team, founded in 1953 by Robert Levy. I was a Little Quaker quarterback.

Jan. 1994, sharing dorm room at W.E.B. DuBois College House, UPenn with family and friends.

2003 2003 SLAM Magazine, Streetball Edition.

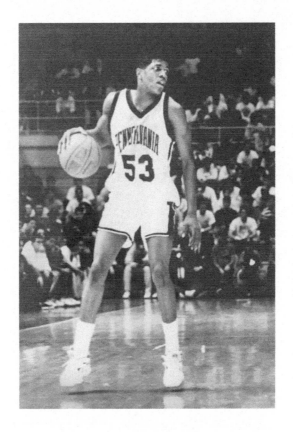

UPenn vs Princeton at The Palestra, sophomore year.

Fall 2000, Rome, with Aida, outside the Colosseum.

Summer, 2004, party at Ebauche En-Vogue salon.

Pre-game, ADR Roma, 2000.

2004, my mom, Janet Nuble, and grandmother, Annie Allen.

JT and Annie Allen, grandparents, Detroit, 1984 .

Fall, 2005, with my sister, Lacresha Allen, in Venice.

March 11, 2015. Final game as head coach at UPenn. Penn vs Princeton.
Players wore #53 for pregame warm-up. Photo by Charles Fox.

NBA Eastern Finals, Cleveland, 2018. Pregame, Game 6, with Terry Rozier.
Photo by Jaime Sabou, Getty Images.

June 2003. HOOD Enriched kids in Rome, outside the Sistine Chapel.

Students from Strawberry Mansion Promise Academy and Camden H.S. visit Harvard's Kennedy School of Government, April 6, 2018.

STEM summer program at Wharton for freshmen and sophomores from Philadelphia schools.

December 30, 2015. Sharing a moment after Kobe's last game at TD Garden.

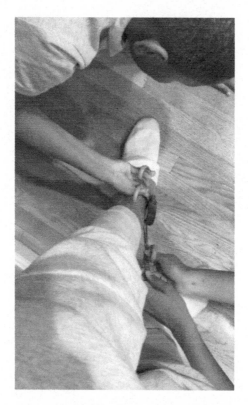

My kids removing the location monitor, Jan. 11, 2020.

January, 2015. Father and son watch Quakers practice.

CHAPTER 20

SEVENTY-TWO HOURS

What a difference a day makes. In my case, what a difference three days made. You see, in a matter of 72 hours, I had gone from sitting on a bench inside a holding cell of a Florida federal prison to sitting on the Boston Celtics' bench for a preseason game vs the Charlotte Hornets. One bench, hard, cold and stiff. The comforts of the other—cushioned, padded and giving. Seventy-two hours, two different benches, two different postures. But the same elephant was in both settings.

I missed the first preseason meeting between the teams two days prior. We departed Boston at 11 a.m. Sept. 27, 2018. Team flights were out of Hanscom's Air Force Base in Bedford, Massachusetts. Like any other road trip, I drove my Black Honda CRV (my soccer mom car, as Evan Turner so politely referred to it) right up to the plane. Valet service removed my luggage from the trunk of the car. I jumped out, showed TSA my ID, and boarded the plane. It was year four for me with the Celtics and I was full and feeling blessed to partake in yet another season in the NBA. Chartered flights, catered meals, per diem and 5-Star hotels—all of this, plus a paycheck? Unreal. What should I ever complain about? And I almost forgot to throw in a front row seat to watch the best athletes in the world perform with grace and flare every night. I'd coach in the NBA for free. As a matter of fact, I should be paying them for allowing me to even have this position.

Nevertheless, I boarded the plane this particular day just like I did for the previous three seasons: thankful, excited and praying for traveling grace. Just plain ole happy to be there. Never would I have imagined that in less than 24 hours, I'd be arrested, booked, fingerprinted, handcuffed, and shackled inside a Florida jail. Alone, cold, confused, afraid, sad, and depressed, I sat there saying, "This can't be real." Actually, it was so real that I thought it really wasn't happening. If I'm making any sense at all.

The flight time from Bedford to Raleigh-Durham was roughly two hours and 25 minutes. Like all the flights during my previous three seasons with the Celtics, I sat in the coaches' section of the plane. It's a Boeing 757 Charter Flight operated by Delta Airlines. The plane is divided into four sections. The front of the plane houses the players. Then a middle common section is reserved for family members (spouses/ kids), and or team corporate sponsors/ partners. The next section holds the coaching staff. And the last section carries anyone from additional staff members, to operations, to local TV and radio analysts. It was a relatively normal flight that day. I say "relatively normal" because I'm well aware of the privileged travel accommodations we're afforded. I've taken a ton of commercial flights. I've run through airports attempting to catch a soon-departing flight. I've been stuck in a TSA line, scared to ask anyone in front of me if I could pass them. "Excuse me, my flight is about to depart. Do you mind if I cut in front of you?" You want to start a fight in an airport? Try jumping the TSA line—people don't care where you're trying to get to, travel rage goes to 10 real quick.

I sat down in the coaches' section. Depending on the time of our flight, I would either order one of two beverages. Early afternoon flights called for a hot tea with lemon and extra sugar. It's a middle of the day beverage, so I'm more relaxed and calmer. Late night, postgame flights usually call for a cup of coffee. I'm either doing a postgame edit, or I'm preparing an edit and report on our upcoming opponent. Headphones on, sipping tea or coffee, listening to one of my home-made mixes, laptop open, locked in. This Charlotte Hornets flight was for the first of our four preseason games. Many teams play preseason games off-site, not at the arena where they play regular season games. We were going to play the Hornets at the Dean Center in Durham, North Carolina.

The flight took off and I began watching footage of our Cleveland series from the 2017-18 Eastern Conference Finals. We lost Game 7 of that series, and it was tough to re-watch. Our team went on a great playoff run, but ultimately came up short. In Boston, it's championship or nothing. The city's nickname is "Titletown." The Bruins, Patriots, Redsox and Celtics—four professional franchises, all with multiple titles. Since the year 2000, the four teams combined have won 12 championships. That means in the past 19 years, the city of Boston has had 12 parades. Us reaching Game 7 of the Eastern Conference Finals, although it was a great accomplishment, it still wasn't good enough in this city.

I actually re-watched the entire series. Our third preseason game this upcoming season was scheduled to be against Cleveland. In prepa-ration for that game, I also glanced over their defensive numbers from that series. I searched for offensive patterns they struggled with through the year, and from our series. Myself, along with one other assistant, were responsible for all of our opponents defensive analysis. Forty-one times a year, we produced edits and reports that break down teams' defensive tendencies. On this day I was locked in, and focused for the entire two hours and 25 minutes. Looking for a slight competitive advantage, with tea in hand, and iPod blasting one of my recorded deejay sets, I settled in.

Our flights have Wi-Fi, but I usually don't turn my phone on until we land. We touched down in Raleigh-Durham, I grabbed my garment bag, stuffed a Gatorade in the side of my backpack, and walked off the plane. The team's coach bus awaited us at the bottom of the steps. I threw my bag underneath and stepped on the bus. We don't have assigned seats, but you know humans are creatures of habit, so I sat my rear end down in the third row. I took a deep breath and turned my phone on. Six message notifications popped up on my screen. Normally, I read them in the order they were received. The only exceptions are when my wife or any of the kids' names pop up. This is evidence I look at the full body of the screen before I do anything. However, when one of the notifications is from your lawyer, you freeze. I instantly broke out into a sweat. No one wants to unexpectedly hear from their lawyer. The news is never good. And although I was anticipating bad news, never did I imagine what was coming.

"Jerome, it's Ron. I tried to call you. I'm not sure if you're traveling with the team right now, but please call me when you get this message. Unfortunately, you have 24 hours to self- surrender. I will fly to Florida to hand you over to the FBI. You have until 11:30 a.m.

tomorrow. I'm sorry, it's actually 10:30 a.m. I'm not sure where you're at right now, but please call me as soon as possible."

Everything stood still. I don't even remember the bus moving. I just remember sitting down on the bus and opening Ron's text. And fast forward, I'm in my hotel room, spread across the bed, staring up at the ceiling. I just left Boston, excited about the start of a new season. I just watched two hours and 25 minutes of film. And now I'm staring at the ceiling trying to wrap my mind around the fact that I'm about to go to jail. In an instant, Raleigh-Durham became the connection to my final destination: I had a date with Wilkie D. Ferguson Jr. U.S. Courthouse in Miami, Florida.

I sat in a chair inside the U.S. Marshall's office wondering to myself, how in the hell I was gonna explain this to my 8-year-old son, among other things. I had on a Hugo Boss dress shirt and a pair of slacks from Zara. Prior to my lawyer handing me over to the FBI that morning, I had to remove my Rolex wristwatch, the Hermes belt that held up my slacks, and the shoelaces from my Allbirds. As best I could, I tried to dress like a middle aged, African American college graduate who's been married to the same woman for 20 years. I really thought my "drippings" would somehow make my exchange with the government and our judicial system smooth, because I didn't look like a convicted felon. Well, tell me what a convicted felon looks like? My garments looked nice, but I had some loose-hanging threads. My exposure had displayed how fragile I was in the seams of my life.

I remember when I bought my first Coogi sweater in college. I wore it every weekend. As a matter of fact, I wore it so much, it could actually walk by itself. One day I noticed it had a thread hanging from the armpit. I tried to pull on it gently enough to keep the garment intact. After the next washing cycle, I had a hole the size of a nickel in that same spot. Not my favorite Coogi! Not my uniform top! The washing machine had challenged the integrity of the garment. Would it hold up at the seams? With the right amount of force, one loose thread destroyed an entire garment. It uncovered what I had been trying to hide. And that was the fact that I was a broke college student, trying to impress the periphery wearing a holey Coogi sweater.

The clothes I wore that morning were trying to cover the flaws in my character. I was beginning to lose grip of that North Philly toughness I proclaimed to possess. The "I'm from Norf, with an F, was slowly leaking out of its container. I've shamed my family, my alma mater, my city, my friends, my teammates, my neighborhood, and the organization I currently work for. The kind-hearted, humbly swagged-out husband and father of four, who's an Ivy League graduate and a member of the largest Baptist church in Philly, just got fingerprinted and booked. It can't be. I'm the City's own, who's also ghetto-fluent in Italian. Not me. My children will lose everything. No more private schools, no more family vacations. The Celtics are going to fire me. I won't be welcomed back at Penn. I've let Aida and the kids down. They are gonna view me as a failure. How could I put their future in jeopardy? How could I be so stupid? I thought I was helping and all I was doing was hurting. The kids will get trolled on social media. No longer will they have access to middle class privileges. I've completely disrupted their sense of normalcy. I've failed former teammates, former coaches and former mentors. I've failed all who've invested in my trajectory over the years. My mother worked tirelessly to push my sister and I out of the cycle of poverty. And here I am, one generation removed from those struggles and with one decision, I've forced my bloodline back into the bullshit.

People only want marginal returns on their investments. The expenditures of time, money and or resources sometimes force separate parties into nonverbal contracts that govern the exchange. That minimum expected return could be captured by this simple statement, "Just don't fuck it up." Too many silent agents in my life extended the aforementioned advice in order for me to propel forward. I thought about Mel Kilgore, Robert Johnston, James Flint, Tennis Young and Dan Dougherty. I thought about all the men who coached me in youth leagues and throughout high school. I thought about all the conversations that took place in car rides after games. I thought about the trips to Wendy's and the spaghetti dinners. I thought about all the church services, and the countless "off the clock" workout sessions.

I thought about every interaction I ever had with these men. They all were heaven-sent. All of them just showed up in my life at the right time. All of them just gave, serviced and invested, with no strings attached. Even when I displayed ungratefulness, and or arrogance, they continued to give. As a matter of fact, the more defiant I was, the tighter they wrapped their arms around me. So when I showed up to the Logan PAL Center drunk after school one day, Officer Kilgore started taking me to church with him—every Sunday. Or when I was stealing Coca Cola sodas out of the office at Gustine Lake Recreation Center, Robert Johnston called Episcopal Academy and got me switched from public to private school. Officer Kilgore drove from Bear, Delaware, to Philadelphia every Sunday to pick me up. And Mr. Bob helped me get into a school that cost $25,000 a year to attend in 1987. Hell, my mom only made $11,000 a year. One made spiritual deposits, the other shifted my educational trajectory. How could I not stay connected to their original investments? They planted seeds and actually witnessed a harvest. It would be hard for either one of them to see the tree they helped plant dry up and stop producing fruit. But here I was, sitting on a cold steel bench inside a federal prison, with shackles on both my ankles and wrists.

CHAPTER 21

CORRECT HISTORICAL PERSPECTIVE: EUROPE

The truest measure of classic is having the ability to stand the test of time. Father Time is undefeated, so what timeline do you use, or rather, what metric do you apply when you deem the relevance of something as classic? Do the details of the metric formulate a classic institution? Or is it arbitrary? By committing to being a life-long learner, can one keep themselves relevant, no matter what the cycle of public taste is? This does not mean the original formula should be ignored, as the seasons change. But by being less married to efforts of the past, you allow yourself to be in tune with current norms. Humans are calculated control freaks—we are drunk off the illusion of planning power. The spirit of the journey, however, won't allow the body of the journey to be predetermined. That's like completely removing our ability to breathe.

We set goals, we have dreams, we have aspirations. But in between pronunciation and maturation, life happens. And the correct historical perspective, as the events of life transpire, will determine whether or not you reach those goals and or dreams. Mental markers allow your personality range to encompass passion, pain, and progress. Will your passion allow you to endure the pain of failure? Will you process pain and failure well enough to learn from your experiences and push forward? These questions essentially mandate that we possess the correct historical perspective when evaluating our own lives. It's as simple as remembering your own story. Then and only then can we apply valuation, or rather make sense of our present positions. Remembering your own story allows you to get closer to purpose. Remembering your own story helps you understand your current story.

I've traveled to numerous places, both domestically and internationally. I really did have to get more pages added to my passport. I've been to Los Angeles, New York City, Miami, Las Vegas, Spain, France and Italy. I've also been to Richard Allen Projects, 8th and Butler and Tasker Homes in Philadelphia. I've eaten surf and turf, and I've eaten government cheese. I've eaten late night from the Chinese store on the Ave and I've eaten late night from outdoor cafes on Via Veneto in Rome. I've shopped on Rodeo Drive in Beverly Hills, on Champs-Elysees in Paris, on Via Condotti (Piazzi di Spagna) in Rome, in the Dumo section of Milan, and at the Grand Bazaar in Istanbul. I've also shopped at the Gallery, City Blue, and on every avenue and street that's deemed an urban central consumption district in Philadelphia. Places like 52nd Street, 5th Street, Erie Avenue and Germantown & Chelten. I've drank Henny in "hood bars" like Wills on 24th Street and Lou and Choose on Hunting Park Avenue, and in velvet rope joints like The Gate in LA and Bar Fly in Paris.

I've lived in North Philadelphia, Montgomery County and in the south of Italy (Napoli). I've lived in a house with 18 other people, and I've lived alone. I had a SEPTA TransPass, and I've had a

Mercedes-Benz. I've had a Granada, and I've had a Range Rover. I went to bed hungry, and I went to bed full. I've had money, and I've been broke. I've attended public school, and I've attended private school. Some things I've done only because that's all my resources would allow me to do. Others I did to either purchase status, or to recapture a wonder.

One of my fondest memories as a child was when I took the train to the movie theater at 15th and Chestnut. Me, Smoke, and Terry went to go see "Krush Groove." Afterward, we ate at Roy Rogers, and then we went to the arcade. Inside the arcade, we waited in line so that we could take a "flick" inside the photo booth. That was the thing to do: go downtown to the arcade and take a picture before you spent all your money. I still have the photo from that day. I had on a Police Athletic League baseball hat and a Villanova Starter jacket, with a five-dollar bill and six ones splattered across my chest. I was balling, baby!

I have a picture of me and my girlfriend (who is my wife now) hugging one night, as the Eiffel Tower illuminated the background. We were walking the streets of Paris on New Year's Eve night. Both of us 24 years young, aimlessly strolling, without a worry in the world. Until it was time to catch a taxi back to the train station. That's when I realized the color of my skin will dictate or determine my ability to successfully solicit a taxi in any global metropolitan hub. I was fine but my girlfriend wanted to amputate her own feet after that three and a half-hour walk in heels, back to the train station.

I also remember walking around the ancient ruins of Pompeii. For the 2004 Christmas holiday, Jerome II and Taylor came to visit me in Napoli, Italy. Their 3rd-grade social studies class was studying Western Civilization. One of the stock photos used in their class depicted what Mount Vesuvius' eruption in 79 AD did to the City of Pompeii. My flat was a 30-minute drive from the display of the remains of this occurrence. When the twins arrived that Christmas holiday, Aida and I took them to visit the piece of history they were currently studying in school. Thinking of the 4,489 miles that separated the classroom observation of the same space injected me with a gigantic dose of gratitude. The game of basketball had us walking the streets of Pompeii in real time.

CHAPTER 22

CORRECT HISTORICAL PERSPECTIVE: HACKMAN

Growing up as a child, there were two things I hated: going to the supermarket and going to the laundromat. The distance between my house and the neighborhood supermarket was 0.7 miles. That's a three-minute drive, or a 14-minute walk. Neither my mom nor my grandparents owned a car, so every road taken by the people in my house was traveled either by public transportation or on foot. I would cry every first of the month, hoping my mother would force one of my older cousins to accompany her to the supermarket. She would always say my tears meant nothing to her. And that I was quick to cry, but even quicker to eat her food. I will admit, though, once those bags hit the door, the entire house lit up—not just me. It was amazing. One person would announce that my mom was back from the supermarket, and instantly, 16 people would fly down the staircase to meet her and help with the bags. The staircase would look as jammed as the fictitious riot Cedric The Entertainer jokingly referred to when he said, "Get Lisa and them."

I on the other hand, would barely make it through the door, hands numb and shoulders detached. You see, at 7 years old, walking 0.7 miles with 10-pound weights in each hand wasn't a pleasant calorie-burning exercise. It was torture on the body. I'd be in so much pain that by the time we arrived home, I forgot I was even hungry. The only thing I wanted to do was lay down on the floor. It was sad, too. Because no one would come to my rescue. The rest of the house would just step over me—and sometimes on me—like I was a throw rug or something. I guess that's what happens when there's a riot: people get trampled.

When we stood in line at checkout, I would always ask my mom if we could save enough money to catch the trolley home, instead of walking. She'd always say it was good exercise for both of us. Every so often she'd get annoyed by my persistent request to take the trolley. And that's when the truth would come out. "Boy, which one are you worried about? Your stomach, or your arms? The money we would spend catching the trolley could go toward another box of Captain Crunch." And that instantly shut me up. She knew I loved Captain Crunch cereal.

So I would put my head down and start swinging my arms around like that of a relief pitcher before entering a baseball game. She knew I'd give my right arm for another box of Captain Crunch. The funny thing is, though, she never brought an extra box, but the thought that she had the ability to buy anything extra left me with a sense of duty. My stomach, our house, the family, needed me to not take public transportation in the name of Crunch Berry. What I didn't know was that she spent every dime she had—I mean every dime—trying to help feed the other 18 people living in my grandparents' house. So after checkout, off we went, four bags in each hand, down a slight hill for .7 miles. I complained so much that I allowed my pain to blind me from the fact that she was carrying double the amount of bags I had. To this day, I marvel at the strength of that woman.

One day, as my mother and I walked out of the supermarket, I noticed an older gentleman blurting out the same phrase over and over again. As every female exited the market, he'd say, "Hackman, Hackman, Hackman." He said it three times to every female that pushed a cart past him. I thought he was a pimp, and this was the new catch phrase females were answering to. But no one responded. Maybe he was an old playa and his lines were outdated. I was confused. Hackman is the call, but he's not getting any love. I definitely knew my mom wasn't going to respond, because she was my mom and she had class.

As our cart approached this man, he locked eyes with my mom and said it again, "Hackman, Hackman, Hackman." Only this time, it seemed his delivery was slow and sensual. Almost as if he was pulling my mom in close to whisper in her ear. If I thought I had to warm my arms and shoulders up to get ready to carry bags, this time I was warming up to get ready to throw some punches. I wasn't going to let him disrespect my mom. The slo-mo utterance of his call picked up pace, the closer he got to her ear. I could feel the tears of anger pile up at the bottom of my eyelids. I was ready to swing. And then she responded to him.

"I don't have any money for a ride, but my mom is frying chicken gizzards, you can come inside and get something to eat." I was confused. Here's a stranger, who appears to be coming on to her, and she invited him to our house? What was going on? I instantly started crying. The cause of these tears, however, wasn't because of anticipated combat. I couldn't believe she would invite this old pimp playa to our house. No, not my mom. She's an angel. She would never indulge in any promiscuous behavior.

"Mom, who is that man and why are we walking towards his car?" She told me his name was Mr. Willie and that he lived around the corner from us. I asked why he kept screaming Hackman at every lady that walked out of the market. She said, "Because that's what he is—a Hackman." As inquisitive 7-year-olds are, I remained true to form, asking another question, tears streaming down my cheeks, "Mom, what's a Hackman?"

Again, she got annoyed and began to threaten me. "Well, if you want, your ass can walk home, I'm getting a ride to the house from Mr. Willie, the Hackman. You keep bugging me about why we getting in the car with a stranger. I know you hate walking with all those bags, so I figured I'd offer Mr. Willie food instead of the $3 he normally charges. And your ass is still complaining. Boy, get yo ass in this car, before I give you something to really cry about."

Hacks were non-descript taxis. They would use their personal cars and park outside supermarkets or at avenue shopping districts and offer rides to transits. Most of the men were from the surrounding neighborhood. They posted at these establishments as if they were full-time employees. Today we would refer to the service as using Uber. It's been in existence for decades in certain communities. Because of innovation and access, someone came along and scaled out the Hackman concept. Just think, you need a ride, you pull out your phone, punch in your desired destination and you actually get into the car of a complete stranger. This used to be a community's only source of transportation.

Mr. Willie figured out how to service a need. The barter, the exchange, be it food or money, predates the existence of Uber.

The intersection of innovation and access brings humor to forced evolution. In 2020 we use Uber; in 1980 we used the Hackman. Our community didn't have the resources to scale it out, or the infrastructure to develop a business plan. Innovation out of poverty—the will, the creativity to find a way, produced this informal labor force. Uber drivers aren't employees of the company. They are independent contractors. This very concept of getting in cars with strangers just made me applaud and appreciate the never recognized think tanks within socio-economically challenged communities.

I even think about the legacy of our cuisines. Some of my ancestors were given scraps: pig intestines, pig feet, pig ears, chicken livers. Those cuts of meat were in their diets. I was asked why everybody in my house growing up as a child ate chitlins but not me. I couldn't get past the smell. When my grandmother boiled them, the entire house turned upside down. I can't eat anything I can smell. Even if I could have gotten past the smell, just knowing that they were the intestines of a pig would make me gag. I wouldn't even carry the bucket that held those contents on my .7 mile walk back from the supermarket. My grandma would always say, "Boy the pig has been good to us. Now run to the store 'cuz your momma forgot the hot sauce." If she were alive today, I'd tell her to call an Uber and go get her own hot sauce.

CHAPTER 23

CORRECT HISTORICAL PERSPECTIVE: MY FIRST TIME

Having the correct historical perspective when evaluating the present moment requires you to sit still. You have to sit still long enough so that the mind is jogged but not altered. One of the greatest gifts we have is the gift of memory. Memory can inspire and encourage. Memory can give direction. I'm thankful for what I remember and for what I don't. Some things are meant to be forgotten. They may possess toxic waste that hinders progression. Sometimes what's forgotten is needed and we choose not to sit still. So I applaud the fruit of needed memory, while being totally aware that my clapping should also be for what's forgotten. The one element of memory that's damn near impossible to forget however, is the phenomenon of first time.

Everyone remembers their first time. Well, I remember my first of many. I remember my first bicycle. I remember the first day the training wheels came off. I remember the first time I drove a car without adult supervision. I remember the first time I smacked the backboard on a layup. I also remember the first time I dunked on a 10-foot basket. I remember my first fight at school. And I remember the first fight I lost. I remember the first date I went on and the first girl I ever kissed. I even remember the first girl I ever brought a gift for. I also remember the first pair of Jordans my mom brought me. I remember my first pair of LEE two-tone jeans and my first pair of patent leather Adidas. I remember the first house party I went to. I even remember the first cassette tape I purchased. I remember the first time I heard Notorious BIG. And I remember my first boom box. I remember attending my first rap concert.

And I remember the first NBA game I played in. I remember my first game playing in Europe. I remember watching a NCAA Tournament game for the first time. And I remember receiving my first college scholarship offer. I remember watching a roach crawl up the wall on my first college home visit. I remember my first crush, and I remember my first bout with rejection. I remember the birth of my first child. And I remember the first time I met my wife. We've all experienced firsts—some more meaningful than others. If we tried to rank our firsts in terms of significance, I'm quite sure the internal battle with self wouldn't allow us to settle on an exact order, probably because we continue to experience firsts as days are afforded to us.

I asked each one of my kids if they remember their first time on an airplane. Jerome and Taylor's first flight took them from Philadelphia to the frigid winter of Minneapolis, Minnesota. They were born Sept. 22, 1995. In December of that same year, exactly at the three-month mark, they boarded a plane to spend the Christmas holiday with me. Jordyn was born Jan. 28, 2002, at Salvator Mundi International Hospital in Roma, Italy. Three months into her existence on earth, she too took her first plane ride. Like the twins, she had no recollection of the nine-hour flight across the Atlantic Ocean. And Roman was two and a half when he first hopped on an Airbus. Penn was playing at Duke University over winter break and my entire family flew from Philadelphia to Raleigh-Durham. Although he was much older than the other three when he took his first flight, Roman didn't remember anything about his first experience, either.

I, however, remember my first time flying. I was 15 years old, and I was an unaccompanied minor flying from Philadelphia to Fort Lauderdale, Florida. I was afraid, nervous, and excited. My mother had never been on a plane, so she couldn't give me any travel pointers. I'm not sure if any of the other 18 people who lived in our house had ever been on an airplane. I was headed to Florida by myself because the rest of the travel party had left the day before. I couldn't depart with them because I had a basketball game. It wasn't a typical rec league game, though. It was Positive Images' first AAU tournament. High School players, freshman through seniors, from the tri-state area packed Philadelphia's Gustine Lake Recreation Center on this partic-ular weekend.

Every recruiting service and every scout lined the walls of this shoebox of a gym to see the likes of Rasheed Wallace from Philadelphia and Donyell Marshall from Reading go head to head. Many arrived early so that they could decide on their own if Luther Wright from Elizabeth, New Jersey, was the most dominant center in the area. Scouts wanted to see Kareem Townes, the young, 6-foot-3 silky smooth scorer from South Philly; they wanted to see if he was the next coming of Lionel Simmons. All was going to be decided this weekend. Many would hold on to their perspectives as truth, and then transfer, without bias, their narratives to the world that consumes high school basket-ball. I must admit, I wasn't on the same level as those other players. But

I needed to be thrown into the fire just so I could gauge for myself how much more work I had to put in to close the gap—or if closing the gap was even possible. The director of the group traveling to Florida knew how important this weekend was to me, so he made concessions to allow me to meet the group the following day. It would be my first time on an airplane.

As we were descending, the lady sitting next to me on the plane told me that the big white things we were approaching were clouds and that planes can fly through clouds. I thought we were about to crash. I closed my eyes and held her hand, and when we broke through the clouds, I saw nothing but water. We approached Fort Lauderdale along the eastern coast of the state. I went from being afraid of the clouds, to damn near urinating on myself because of the water. I thought we were headed for a nosedive right into the ocean. So when my kids flipped the question and asked me if I remembered my first time flying I said, "Yes, I remember. I was 15 years old and I thought I was about to die—two times."

In 1953 a youth football organization was created in the Germantown section of Philadelphia. Its mission was to provide young boys from the Delaware Valley with a football experience that mirrored those at both the collegiate and professional level. Their deliverables would be manifested through intentional exposure. These youth would travel all across the country playing against some of the nation's best in their age bracket. A 22-year-old UPenn graduate would name this organization the Philadelphia Little Quakers. Although he played tennis in college, his passion and love for the game of football would be expressed through the opportunities he afforded others. Some 35 years after the conception of this organization, I too would benefit from the generosity and passion of Robert Levy.

I'll never forget my first time flying; more importantly, I'll never forget Robert Levy. The class of 1952 graduate would go on to be a trustee at the University for over 40 years. He was the founder of the Little Quakers.He introduced me to economy class, and he introduced me to the University of Pennsylvania. There's so much irony around this. The Little Quakers was founded in 1953. My mom was born in 1953. The organization was located in Germantown. By the time I was selected to play for the football team in 1988, my family had moved from North Philadelphia to the Germantown section of the city. My first time on Penn's campus was for a Little Quakers scrimmage. I had never been to that part of the city. I didn't know where Franklin Field was and I was completely oblivious of the fact that we were on UPenn's campus.

Even when I decided to attend Penn after my senior year of high school, I did so without ever visiting the school. I didn't make the connection until after I arrived for my freshman year. Robert Levy was responsible for several of my firsts. Twenty-two years after our initial meeting, he also was the first person to call me after I became the John R. Rockwell Head Coach of Men's Basketball at the University of Pennsylvania.

In the Fall of 2010, I attended a reception inside a tennis pavilion on UPenn's campus. This event was the athletic department's attempt to thank all the donors for their contributions to the recent capital campaign fund. Our AD raised $125 million in an effort to change the aesthetics of the eastern-most part of Penn's campus. Their contributions helped extend the campus to the banks of the Schuylkill River.

Softball fields, outdoor tennis courts, soccer fields and a retractable bubble—all would change the landscape of one of the nation's most prestigious universities. Needless to say, the athletic department went "all-out" for this dinner. They converted this indoor tennis facility into an elegant landing spot fit for kings and queens. Awards, acknowledgements, and thank you's were the backdrop for the evening. I must say, it was masterfully planned. People who have philanthropic dispositions more often give not because they want to be acknowledged (although secretly, they hope to be), but rather, they're motivated to give because they care. And judging from the amount of money that this capital campaign raised, a ton of people cared about Penn Athletics.

This was the first time I had attended such an event. I was entering my first full season as the John R. Rockwell Head Coach of Men's Basketball. The athletic department gave 33 intercollegiate sports teams the platform to compete, and all 33 head coaches were required to attend this dinner. It was an exhausting, but special night for me. Previously, I had been an assistant coach under Glen Miller for only three months. After we started the season with a 0-7 record, the AD decided to make a change midseason. And on December 11, 2009 I was asked to head the program on an interim basis. We finished the season 8-20. However, the following April, the AD removed the interim tag and I was awarded a four-year contract.

So, the night inside the tennis pavilion was pretty much my first formal event with the "big dawgs." I think I spoke with every person in attendance. I even spent several minutes talking to the bartender. If intoxication was your desired deliverable for the evening, he was the most important person in the room. If Penn Athletics and the state of the department's flagship sport was your primary concern, then I was the point person for that conversation. I really only wanted to talk to the bartender, though. Not because I wanted to hydrate myself, or because I was intimidated by the room. I just felt comfortable talking to the bartender because he was my older brother. He worked for the catering company that was hired for the event. I was forced to move away from his station because the celebrated guests of the evening wanted my undivided attention.

What they didn't realize was that, if it wasn't for the bartender, I would not have been standing in front of them that day. He taught me how to drive a car. He would take public transportation to watch my high school games. He gave me money for haircuts. He took me to play tennis. He made sure I didn't succumb to the stakes of our neighborhood. His mother and my mother were sisters. He was my cousin by blood but my big brother at heart. And on this night, no one else recognized the significance of the bartender.

My exhaustion didn't come from "kissing babies" like a politician, even though I was solicited by more than half the room. I'd played college basketball for the very same program I now was coaching. While playing at Penn, I was fortunate to be a part of three Ivy League Championship teams. Several of my teammates and I were voted All-Ivy Players. In 1994 we won a first round game in the NCAA Tournament. Our group won 42 consecutive conference games over a three-year span. Many of the individuals in attendance remembered the teams from that era. It was humbling to be coaching at my alma mater. And it was even more humbling to receive such an outpour of support from damn near the entire room. It was the first time I represented the University and the program in a gala format. How fitting is it to say, the name of the facility hosting the event that evening was the Robert P. Levy Tennis Pavilion.

CHAPTER 24

SNOWSTORMS

When James Harden and the Houston Rockets came to town Sunday, March 3, 2019, the entire New England area was bracing for a Nor'easter. Not quite like the storms of 2015, though. But any snowfall in the month of March feels like a Nor'easter since spring fever is knocking at the door that time of the year.

I remember riding through Cambridge in February 2015. Snow piles looked like baby mountains. I had never seen anything like it, let alone attempted to drive through it. Our coach bus couldn't make it down the streets of Allston. Cars were covered, literally covered. We exited Mass Pike in route to the team's hotel, and all of our players' heads turned like tourists sightseeing. It was late Thursday night. We'd departed Penn's campus six hours earlier, thinking we'd arrive in Cambridge without any hiccups. Never did we think Mr. Bruce, our bus driver, would have to turn down the soulful tunes of the Temptations, soothingly coming through our bus speakers, because he would need complete silence in order to navigate the snow-covered streets of Metro Boston. From Jan. 24, 2015, to Feb. 22, 2015, Boston received 94 inches of snow. It was a record 30-day snowfall.

The anticipated snowfall for the March 2019 day the Celtics would face the Rockets was 6 to 8 inches; however, close to 15 inches ended up falling on the region. Dense flakes started descending slightly after our Rockets game tipped off. The March snow poured on our normalcy at the same rate that James Harden poured his 42 points on our defenders. And it continued to snow well into the next day, Monday. Most of the ground and air transportation was suspended for the area. Boston's Logan International Airport canceled all inbound and outbound flights. There was a small window between 5 a.m. and 8 a.m. Sunday, when they allowed a couple of flights to depart. Outside of that, nothing—no movement at Logan. Passengers were fighting to beat the storm and get out of town. Flights were overbooked. And plenty of backpacks became pillows as people were forced to camp out in the airport.

The Celtics were scheduled to take a postgame flight to San Francisco immediately following Sunday's game versus the Rockets. Going west for most Eastern Conference teams usually requires a minimum two days in between travel and actual game. Since I've been with the team, we have never flown to California the day before a scheduled game. Leaving Sunday postgame was fitting for our upcoming Tuesday contest versus the Golden State Warriors. There was one problem though: the approaching storm. Logan was already shut down, and even though the snowfall wouldn't be heavy by the end of our game, Team Operations wasn't sure if we could de-ice in enough time to fly away from the storm. Departing Hanscom didn't mean we were completely independent of Logan. But it did give us the autonomy to at least load up and try to depart.

I was in panic mode. Not because I was afraid to fly in a snow-storm; but rather, because I had a separate itinerary from the team. I was scheduled to fly from Logan International to Miami International Airport on Sunday after our game. I had a mandated court appearance the next morning inside Wilkie D. Ferguson Federal Courthouse. My plans were to fly to Miami after our game, and then join the team either late Monday night or early Tuesday morning. Golden State was my offensive scout, so I was hoping everything went smoothly and I could present my video edit right before tipoff. Simple and easy: fly in, fly out, hop in an Uber and be at the hotel either late Monday or before shootaround Tuesday morning. But here comes the Nor'easter. No plan B, no conditions in place for inclement weather.

As it got close to Sunday, I had to make a decision to either leave several days before the storm would arrive or leave right before it started. I felt good about playing it close, even though my entire life depended on me being in court Monday. How crazy is that? But I was warned that the trial was running longer than scheduled and that I could possibly be in Florida for a couple of days. I'm a "glass is half full" type of guy, an optimist. So I said things will work out. I'll miss the bad weather, I'll fly out Sunday evening, get to court Monday, tes-tify, and be on the Airbus Monday night. I wasn't trying to miss any games. I still was amazed by the Celtics' understanding and patience throughout my entire ordeal, and I didn't want to take it for granted. So leaving early and missing the Rockets game was something I wasn't trying to do. And there was a possibility that I might not be called to take the stand right away. Naw, I'll be on the bench for the game and fly out afterwards.

All commercial flights suspended Sunday. What the heck was I going to do? How am I going to get to Miami? I could drive south to another city after the game and then try to fly out from there. I could take Megabus. What the fuck am I going to do? I couldn't call the Assistant Attorney General's office and say, "Umm, I'm stuck in Boston. I'll catch y'all the next time." They were expecting me. They had witnesses lined up, and the trial was already extended past their desired timeline. The last thing I wanted to do was mess up their flow. I was shook. I sat in the coaches' locker room, face planted in the palm of my hands, head pounding, stressed out.

I had only one option, and even that wasn't certain. I could fly from Boston to San Francisco with the team after the game, and then fly from San Francisco to Miami when we get there. That was the only way I could get there in time. But it still wasn't established whether or not the team's Boston to San Francisco flight was definitely taking off. If I didn't get to Miami before they were ready to call me as a witness, I was gonna get roofed. "Lord, please let our flight take off. I don't care about the quick turnaround. Just let me get to that courthouse in time."

I was already nervous about taking the stand. I had never been in a courtroom before, and to be honest, although I was going to admit only to what The Alphabet already had proof of, I still was uneasy about it. Most of it stemmed from the code—you know, the code in the hood. Me, taking the stand—I might get labeled a rat. They had the proof, and I didn't deny it. I couldn't deny it. They did their home-work before they indicted me. They don't waste the government's time or resources. How I would be viewed by my neighborhood was one concern. Not making it to court was on a completely different level of preoccupation. Aida kept asking me why I was so worried. She said those who were connected to the case were worried about one thing and one thing only – themselves. She told me they didn't have a problem steering The Alphabet in my direction to begin with. She kept saying, "OK, you think all your friends and associates have your or your family's best interest in mind? You better think again."

I grew up in North Philly, and I was raised by Old Heads who taught us to stand what we did: don't blame anyone, and don't point fingers. I thought that was a universal truth. I remember when our next-door neighbor got stabbed in the chest for stealing someone's bike. He knew who stabbed him, but he refused to tell the police when they showed up. I accepted the money. I wanted the buck to stop with me. I wasn't trying to bring others into the fold just because I got caught. I did it. And I didn't have any problems admitting that—it was just that getting to the location of my admittance caused uneasiness.

It might have been the first time in my professional coaching career that I wasn't concerned about the results of a game. As coaches, we try to grade every play, every win, and or every loss the same. At any given point in the season, it's our job to truly evaluate where our respective teams stand. After losses, we tend to look a little deeper, even though bad wins can trick you into masking success. I try and peel back layers, especially after a loss. But after this loss, I was thinking about one thing and one thing only: will our team plane takeoff? We lost that game on Sunday, March 3, 2019, and James Harden scored 42 points. He dazzled the crowd at T.D. Garden with step back after step back. I went to chapel before the game like I always did, and Reverend Gray used Philippians 4:7 to set the atmosphere for this gathering. In the midst of him reciting the verse, I just started smiling. God knew what I needed to hear: "And the peace of God which surpasses all understanding will guard your hearts and your minds in Christ Jesus."

Hearing those words allowed me to be present on the bench that night. I was able to support and encourage, in voice and in silence. And although we lost, Rev's words changed my lens. Whether or not our plane took off or not wasn't up to me or my worries. If the snowstorm didn't allow any departures, the government would understand. The tension I carried about every interaction with The Alphabet almost caused me to lose my mind. But when the captain announced the flight time and for us to fasten our seat belts, I couldn't help but quietly say, "Thank you, Jesus."

Six hours and four minutes later, we landed at SFO. The 32-minute bus ride from SFO to our lodging got us in the Four Seasons Hotel at 1a.m. I showered, got under the bedsheets, set the alarm on my iPhone for 3 a.m. and went to sleep. I hadn't slept the entire plane ride. In the event I didn't make it back to San Francisco for the Warriors game, I wanted to at least make sure all of my scout material was buttoned up. By the time I was ready to fall asleep, we were preparing to land. So after a hot shower, I was ready to pass out. And pass out I did—for two whole hours. My body was still on East Coast time; therefore, it was easy to wake up after my "power nap." I jumped in an Uber and was back at SFO for a 5 a.m. flight to Miami International Airport. Four hours and forty-six minutes, back across the country. Suit on, tie inside my sports coat, with a lightly stuffed backpack. I anticipated a short stay. It was 11 hours, more or less, of air travel, all because of a snowstorm. From Boston to San Francisco to Miami— even Spirit Airlines wouldn't give you this type of connection. The route didn't matter, however; I was just grateful that I made it to the Wilkie D. Ferguson Federal Courthouse by Monday, March 4, 2019.

CHAPTER 25

CHOCOLATE CAKE

Where I am weak, He is strong. He kept me standing, He kept me smiling. When the world undressed me, He kept me covered, kept my wife covered, kept my children fed. He kept me in good counsel. He kept me employed. I owe a lot to the Boston Celtics. They allowed me to walk into arenas while a thorn was sticking out of my pant leg. Like the thorn that stuck out of the Apostle Paul's side, mine too was a reminder of God's grace and mercy. I sat on the front row, right next to arguably one of the brightest basketball minds in the game today, with a location monitor strapped around my ankle. All of my suits' pant legs are cut tight at the ankle. It's the Italian influence I adopted after living there for eight years. At times, you could see the black box bulging out. Sometimes, when I stood up during a timeout, my pant leg would get caught on top of the monitor.

And yet, I still was allowed to coach, I still was allowed to assist, I still was allowed to service. Never in the history of this league has a coach sat on a NBA bench with a location monitor around his ankle. That's nothing but God. I can't take any credit for it. He placed me in an organization, and around an ownership group that epitomized the true meaning of compassion. They saw me for who I was, while acknowledging what I did. They not only cared about me, they cared about my family. I get emotional every time I think about it. I don't think any other organization in this league would have wrapped their arms around me like this organization did. And that speaks volumes about the type of individuals running this franchise.

At times my flesh wanted to peek its head out. Like when I was informed that I was removed from the Penn Athletics Hall of Fame. Or when I received a 15-year ban from the NCAA. Or when my own cousin called me a rat. Part of my body would jerk forward because it wanted to respond. I'm human. But I never lost complete control, because in the end, the exposure made me better. I was asked if I could do it all over again, would I make different choices. I paused. I wasn't quite sure how to respond. Part of me remembers how taxing this whole ordeal was on my family and the University. So I would respond by saying, "Yes, I would make different/better choices." The other part of me, however, feels like I'm better because of it all. I now know God like I've never known him before. My walk, my testimony, is stronger, is deeper. You don't reach this point without going through what I went through.

Selfishly speaking, I like where our relationship is at now—and it took for this to happen for me to get here. So I'm not quite sure how to answer that question. I'm torn. The reality of it all is that, my failure in character, my integrity not matching the platform I was given, forced me into a season where it was just me and God and no one else. Now though, I hope that people look at me, look at my transparency, look at my service, look at my brokenness, look at my smile, and look at my posture and say, God is truly awesome!

I let Roman and Jordyn cut the location monitor off my leg. They both were excited when my 180 days were completed. Jordyn made plans to do it at the 12:01 a.m. mark the night before, but I fell asleep by 10:30 that evening. Each one had a pair of scissors, and they were arguing over who was going to do it. I decided to let both of them cut it off at the same time, from two different angles. Watching them remove the monitor gave me so much strength. Throughout the exposure, my main concern wasn't how the rest of the world would view me, but rather, if this would change the lens of Aida and the kids in regard to me. For 22 years, Aida had loved and supported me unwaveringly. We had been through so much, and yet and still she never lost sight of her dedication to her marriage. She knew everything about me, both good and bad. I tried to shield my kids from my mistakes and brokenness. All their lives, I tried to let their fairytale perceptions of their dad reign. But my exposure killed that fiction; it's like that old saying, "When heroes fall, hero-worshipers fall even harder." I was worried that them seeing me as less than would somehow make them feel inadequate. But Roman and Jordyn did two things the day I got off house arrest that made me feel superhuman. The first was the excitement they embraced while cutting the monitor off my leg. They felt like they were freeing their dad. The second took place later that evening at dinner.

Being on house arrest meant I had movement restrictions. I was allowed to drive the kids to school in the morning, go to work and perform community service. My probation officer also allowed functional duties that included but weren't limited to doctor's appointments, grocery shopping, and attending the kids' local athletic competitions. That was pretty much my norm anyway. However, when you know you have to be in the house by a certain time, you carry a certain amount of anxiety. For home games held at T.D. Garden, I had a threshold of

12:30 a.m. Postgame staff meetings, triple overtime games, or post-game meals all had to be wrapped up in enough time so that I made it home by then. If it was a regular Wednesday, meaning a non-game day, and I had to be in the house by 6 p.m., Roman would get worried if I pushed the envelope. Several times I recall him blurting out from the back of the Honda, "Dad, hurry up, it's almost 6 o'clock." So on my first night off house arrest, I decided to take the kids to dinner after our game.

We typically don't eat late as a family. I especially don't like to eat after 8 p.m. Once you get to be my age, food takes longer to digest, and extra pounds are much harder to shred. If we ever went out late for a meal, usually the atmosphere was of equal importance. Sometimes the late-night dining was all about atmosphere and less about the meal. Having a daughter approaching 18 years of age meant she wasn't in a rush to get home on weekend game nights. So Saturday, after our Pelicans game, with no time restrictions dangling over my head, I decided to take the kids to dinner.

I let Jordyn pick the type of food and the restaurant. She picked Strega in the Seaport District of the city. By the time her, Roman and I arrived, one side of the restaurant was converted into a Ancestry. lounge. The deejay had the bar area dance floor packed. The other side of the restaurant had patrons properly spaced for dining. Roman ordered calamari, Jordyn ordered Shrimp Parmesan, and I ordered a Shirley Temple. Again, it was late and I didn't want anything heavy on my stomach. Plus, this outing wasn't about my hunger. It was all about just doing something I took for granted—spending time with my kids, no matter the location or time of the day. Taylor worked nights in an ICU at Einstein Hospital in Philly, so she couldn't come to Boston this weekend. And Jerome was helping one of his college mentors run a workshop in New York City. Just being out at dinner, watching them eat and laugh, was so filling.

At the conclusion of the meal, right after Jordyn ordered dessert for one, Roman said he had to go to the bathroom. Jordyn jumped up to accompany him. The two of them got up, went to the bathroom, and were seated at the table again, in all of three minutes. We sat at the table bobbing our heads to the tunes coming from the dance floor. I said, "Jordyn, I can't believe you ordered desert this late." She responded, "Chilll, Old Head, let me live." Then, she and Roman started laughing.

As I looked to my right, I could see our waiter approaching the table. He lowered the plate in front of me. It had the garnishments of perfectly sliced strawberries, accenting a single portion of chocolate cake. And with chocolate syrup, the word CONGRATS was drizzled at the top of the plate. Neither one of them had to use the restroom— they got up from the table so that they could go ask the waiter to personalize the desert. It was a celebration for them. They were happy I was off house arrest. I put my head down—my eyes started to fill with tears. I let go of the guilt I was still carrying. They showed me that no matter what, I was always going to be their Old Head.

PART IV

Had you been practicing on your art,
you'd know your way in the dark. Silence, silence.
DRAGON FLY JONES

CHAPTER 26

UNEXPLAINABLE MISSES

I've been fortunate enough to have three of my children go through the college admissions process. I've witnessed both the tears of acceptance and the tears of rejection. The tears of acceptance are connected to the anxious release of a desired outcome. The tears of rejection speak for themselves. No one wants to hear the word no, no one wants to feel inadequate. The reality of it though is that society forces us to think rejection means we're less-than. Like I said, I've had three children apply to colleges—and all three of their SAT scores were separated by 30 points or less. Yet two of them got accepted into an Ivy League school, and one got rejected by an HBCU. Now, how is that possible?

It could possibly suggest that SAT scores are not true indicators of a prospective student's ability to excel in an academic setting. There are systems and criteria in place that hint at the processes for selection not being immune to possessing inconsistencies. Just because a metric has to mirror institutional agendas, doesn't mean it's not flawed. It just means there will be some unfortunate rejections that are unexplainable.

When I first got the Volunteer Assistant position at Penn, there was commentary throughout the league regarding a particular prospective student athlete. He was deemed a top tier academic recruit and all 8 Ivy League schools were trying to get involved. The Patriot League had just started awarding athletic scholarships, so the pool of student/athletes who fit the Ivy League academic profile was shrinking. Not shrinking because they didn't have the grades or talent, but shrinking because, with a change in institutional policy, the financial burden associated with attending a high academic school was removed. Schools such as Boston University, Colgate University and Bucknell College may not hold the brand recognition or prestige of an Ivy but they were now getting the top tier academic recruits that desired to go to Ivies in the past. Families were willing to trade the $250,000 associated with attending an Ivy, with a slightly less prestigious wall decoration. And, some of the Patriot League schools were just as difficult to get into as their Ivy counterparts.

The seven Ivy schools that danced around the recruiting landscape of the aforementioned prospective student athlete could not understand how he found his way onto an Ivy campus. He had previously been rejected by a Patriot League school admission's department. But the same SAT score and the same calculated grade-point average (GPA) allowed him to be admitted to an Ivy League school. This was my first introduction to a complicated and complex college admissions process.

Colleges and universities align their principles, values, and expectations with their core constituents. Nevertheless, it's becoming increasingly harder year after year to compose incoming classes. The world is changing, and tomorrow's students are growing and learning faster than today's students. So, admission formulas aren't exact; they are constantly evolving. Students are competing in a global market.

Which makes Deans' and Admission Directors' jobs the hardest jobs to execute on campus. Deciding who will benefit most from campus space, as well as identifying candidates who will innovatively add value and push the space forward, can't be solely measured by a standardized test score. The score could represent your base, but we must admit to ourselves, there will be some misses.

The trending phrase today is the "holistic student." Grades, scores, activities, community engagement—all these categories support the main indicator. Admission office's dissection of who can and cannot excel at university life will always be a collection of moving parts. Again, your baseline is your baseline, but could someone please explain to me how three kids with the same SAT score, and relatively, the same grade-point average (GPA) be so unevenly qualified that two got into an Ivy and one was turned down by a HBCU?

I can try and take a crack at answering my own question by simply stating, it's complicated. Race, gender, academic fortitude, residential domain, athletic prowess and claims of legacy, all take up computation residency when admission departments start to form incoming freshman classes. On March 23, 2014, Fiona Glisson wrote an article for "The Daily Pennsylvanian" that carried a subtitle that stated that the Class of 2018 was the most competitive class in Penn's history. Including both early and regular decision applicants, of the 35,868 applicants, only 9.9% of the 35,868 who applied were selected. Glisson not only gave the acceptance rate for the Class of 2018, she also included data on gender, residency, SAT scores and legacy as well. Her article stated that the Class of 2018 would have a female composition of 52%, and a legacy declaration of 13%. It also disclosed what percentage of the incoming class were first generation college students, and which state played home to the largest body of accepted students.

She did an awesome job of glossing over the general data commonly shared by universities. Five years later, Penn received 44,961 applicants for admission to the class of 2023. And of that number only 7.7% were offered admission. Penn's applicant pool increased by almost 10,000 applicants, while its acceptance rate has dropped by 2.2%. The data from this sample size supports the appealing stigma of a simple supply and demand chart.

CHAPTER 27

WHAT WOULD YOU DO?

As a parent, ask yourself this question: are you willing to exhaust resources and leverage relationships to help give your child the best educational opportunities possible? Let me be the first to raise my hand and say yes. Technology has made the world small. The byproduct of shrinkage created a competitive pool contained only by cemented global walls. American students no longer rival one another; they are competing globally for jobs, resources and yes, admission slots. We are all citizens of the world now. So paying for SAT prep courses isn't considered a luxury anymore—it's a necessity.

What about those who can't afford private tutoring? I'm aware of the economic disparities mirrored by this country. But as a parent, should I not try and prepare my children to best position themselves in life? My mother couldn't afford to pay $4500 for SAT prep classes. The resources and privilege my children subconsciously own as a birthright have no resemblance to my childhood normalcy. I have a fourth grader who does all of his writing assignments for school on Google Drive— yes, Google Drive. He had to show me how to log in. My high school senior does all of her calculus homework on her iPad (with her iPen).

For four months after I was fired from Penn, I taught at Strawberry Mansion Promise Academy in North Philadelphia. It was rare that students came to class with a writing instrument, let alone something to write on. You want to talk about the gap between the have and the have nots???? And guess what? At the rate that technology is changing the world, the gap is only getting wider.

When my oldest son shared a conversation with me about AI, I initially thought we were about to talk about Allen Iverson. But he was educating me on artificial intelligence, programming, and teaching computers how to think. I shook my head and begged him to slow down his explanation. "You mean to tell me all of this stuff is happening in real time?"

I didn't force my children to take coding classes, or foreign language classes, outside of what their schools offered—and all of them were lifers at independent schools. The conversations they were having in school with some of their friends was eye-opening.

"Wait, you mean to tell me you want me to pay for you to take a Mandarin class? Why can't you take Spanish or French as your foreign elective in school? What, we barely get through the math you're currently assigned in school. It's no way I'm signing you up to take a Russian math class outside of school."

These conversations were taking place before my kids hit sixth grade. The mentality of the families at my kids' school was on another level. My kids stepped into environments where they were either a slight step behind, or at the floor, in terms of exposure. Did that make me a bad parent, or just an uninformed one?

The race to stay on pace—not win, just to stay on pace is stressful for both the parent(s) and the student(s). Suicide rates amongst college students is at an all-time high. Student loan debt in this country is well over a trillion dollars. The cost of education has sky-rocketed, and the percentage acceptance rates at elite colleges and universities are declining. More applicants, not enough slots. It's a little bit of a smoking mirror, if you ask me.

What most people don't know is that I turned down three job offers while I was coaching at Penn. One of the job offers would have quadrupled the salary I was making at the time. It would have paid several millions of dollars over the life of the contract. Annually, I would have made more money than I did during any season I was a pro basketball player. One of the offers held so much prestige that my best friend told me I was crazy for rejecting it. And as much as I wanted to take Greg Popovich up on his offer, I knew, by me being an employee of the University, and possessing a branch of legacy, my children, if they fit the academic profile of a Penn applicant, would have an opportunity to attend the University. If I would have accepted the assistant coach's position with the San Antonio Spurs, the twins' life trajectory would have been altered. I wanted to coach in the NBA, I wanted to sit under the best coach in the history of the game. But more than that, I wanted my children to have access to an elite education.

Sacrifice, leverage and invest—my parental obligation stayed connected to the descriptive responsibilities associated with said title. Private school education, private tutoring, networking, resource building—all to put our children in the best position possible. All to give them the proper educational foundation. All to make sure they become fruit-bearing citizens of the world. I always complained about the cost of independent school tuition. But we wouldn't have it any other way.

When it was time for Jerome II and Taylor to start their college application process, they took two different approaches. Although Taylor applied Early Decision to Penn, she played the totality of the college app process safely by applying to five other schools. Jerome II, on the other hand, didn't even consider safety schools. I begged him to apply to some other schools, even though I felt both he and Taylor stood a good chance at being accepted as a legacy case. Their dad went to Penn and was currently working there as well. I thought they were a sure shot, but you never know until you know.

One day during the waiting period for Early Decision, I got a call from the two of them because one of their fellow classmates at school was walking around with a spreadsheet they made to predict who was going to get into Penn and who was not. Their graduating class had 84 seniors, 19 of whom applied Early Decision to Penn. The spreadsheet highlighted each applicant and his or her connection to Penn. One student had a parent who was a professor at the University, another student had a family member whose name was on a campus building, and Jerome II and Taylor's dad was the coach of the basketball team, and an alum. The level of detail this investigative report contained blew my mind. On the low, they tried to make my kids feel bad, and discredit the legitimacy of their qualification. I told them not to worry about what others thought, and that if the shoe was on the other foot, those same students would take advantage of the connection as well.

I understand firsthand why parents spend time and resources, and leverage platforms and relationships. I wanted to be able to not so much extend legacy to my own children, but rather I wanted to just simply give them an opportunity—an opportunity to attend one of the best universities in the world. No job offer or amount of money could hinder me from transferring access and privilege. Jerome II and Taylor did all the work: they fit the academic profile of a Penn applicant. But the admission process is complicated and forever evolving. Again, I've witnessed the tears of acceptance and the tears of rejection. And although I don't advocate or glorify the role I played in my failure in character, I would like to know if you would be willing to exhaust yourself in any legal expenditure possible to give your child access to the best?

CHAPTER 28

MOMMA GOLDPIECE

The end of WWII helped trigger the start of suburbanization in America. Twelve million soldiers returned home to a housing scarcity. Postwar effects on the U.S. economy catapulted it into a world leader. Industry was booming. New governmental policies and institutions, such as the G.I. Bill and the Federal Housing Administration (FHA), assisted in the creation of a "middle class." Low interest loans, and stipends for college and or trade schools, allowed returning soldiers to strategically plant themselves on trajectories independent of forced urban interaction. FHA's first attempt at creating a gateway to the middle class had failed. Housing projects once reserved for whites-only experienced significant flight, while projects deemed for blacks had long wait lists.

After WWII, America's growth in the auto industry and governmental support for new infrastructure changed previously required consumption locations. Americans were no longer dependent upon urbanized central hubs. What did suburbanization do to the city? For one, industry left. Loss of industry meant loss of jobs. Loss of jobs meant loss of property value. Crime and violence increased, while civil service and economic resources experienced staggering decline. Of the 12 million returning soldiers, some 2 million plus immediately went to college. And of the remaining 9 million or so, 5 million returned home, married, and used the GI Bill to purchase homes in newly created communities outside of the city.

The byproduct of our country's newly acquired global position forced the nation into another war. World War II ended, and the Cold War began. In an attempt to stop the growth of communism, the United States fought to have a more democratic presence throughout the world. Russia, as well as China, rivaled the U.S. on many fronts. And as a result, with neither country willing to suppress their spheres of governing influence, the Cold War would last 45 years. Both countries' desire for global dominance created and influenced subsidiary wars, which have consequential impacts still felt today. The ideological forces of the Cold War were at the center of the Korean War, the Cuban Missile Crisis, and the Vietnam War. The threat of the spread of communism to one Southeast Asian country caused U.S. government officials to employ the services of over 2.7 million Americans in the Vietnam War.

Its nearly 20-year engagement birthed political protests and shaped political campaigns. In an eight-year span, it is said the U.S. government spent well over $120 billion fighting the Vietnam War. Although President Nixon signed the Paris Peace Accords Jan. 27, 1973, ending the Vietnam War, the residue caused by the excessive war expenditure placed economic constraints on the country. This coupled with The Oil Crisis of 1973, sparked inflation and a 400% rise in the price of oil. Its global impact trickled all the way down to a tiny row home in North Philadelphia.

Most of the homes in this section of the city were heated by oil. The neighborhood was once populated by those of Jewish descent, against a backdrop supported by Philadelphia's rich industrial economy. But in 1973, the flight caused by suburbanization left many Jewish families racing for the outskirts. With the failure of housing projects and the influx of southern migrants, a once diverse and socially constructed section of Philadelphia turned into a poverty-stricken, resource-challenged enclave. Glimpses of what once was remained on the 2600 block of North Sixth Street, but the darker pigment of its current residents blocked out any signs of diversity and or prosperity.

In 1973 both of my grandparents worked. Actually, my grandfather had just retired from the Naval Yard. He both served and worked in the Navy for over 30 years. My grandmother worked as a housekeeper for a Jewish family in Montgomery County. Their combined weekly income was $106. Even though their combined yearly income was several thousands of dollars below the national household average, it wasn't bad for a black, working class couple in 1973. But when $106 a week has to cover living expenses for you and 18 of your family members as well, your economic chart tends to depict a steep decline—meaning the more dependents living in my grandparents' house, the less they were able to provide. Back then, a dozen eggs cost $0.78, a gallon of milk cost $1.31. And residential heating oil was $1.73 per gallon. The year before, residential heating oil was only $0.20 per gallon. The shock of a year's jump in price forced many families to reevaluate needs versus wants. So imagine living in a home with a 100 gallon oil tank in the basement and one year only having to pay $20 per week for heat and hot water, and the next year for the same utilities you have an additional $150 weekly spike—that would force any household to prioritize functional capabilities with its residence.

Everybody, I mean everybody, lived at my grandparents' house. The couple emigrated in 1950 from Lincoln, Georgia, to the Frankford section of Philadelphia with four children. Over the course of the next 23 years, they would have an additional three children of their own, and an astonishing 25 grandchildren—all of whom would be raised by them. Coming from strong southern roots where families tended to flock together, this sheltering was not abnormal to my grandparents. Immediately following their wedding ceremony in 1938, they moved into the house of my grandfather's parents. Today, the majority of married couples establish private living quarters to symbolize not only their independence, but also their commitment to one another. This was not the case in 1938. OK, some couples moved out of the "Big House." But most newlyweds stayed on family grounds.

You have to understand the time frame we are talking about. It was 1938 and a 13-year-old girl and a 19-year-old boy were joined in holy matrimony. Both were young and uneducated, so where were they going to go? I asked my grandma about their honeymoon and she replied, "What honeymoon?" She told me that after the wedding ceremony she went to her in-laws' house and played jump rope with her sisters-in-law. She was totally innocent. You would think that a 13-year-old who's married would be considered a fast mover. But this was not the case. Their entire courtship consisted of long talks on my great-great grandmother's porch. No holding hands, and definitely no kissing. And all my grandfather's visits to the house were monitored by my great-great grandmother, Momma Goldpiece.

Momma Goldpiece was the mother of my grandmother's father. My grandmother's mom, whose name was Cora, left my grandmother to be raised by Momma Goldpiece, while she went off to work in

Florida. She always sent money back to help take care of her daughter. And every so often, Cora would return to Lincoln, Georgia, to see her only daughter. But from birth, until the age of 13, Momma Goldpiece was the only mother my grandmother knew.

My grandmother was raised in a three-room ranch where the multipurpose room served as the living room, the dining room and a bedroom. There was another separate bedroom and a kitchen. That's it. Twelve people lived in this house. My grandmother's father, George, had a total of five kids, with my grandmother being the oldest. George's sister, her husband and their three kids. And if you add Momma Goldpiece that would make twelve.

Momma Goldpiece's husband died five years before my grandmother was born. And there are conflicting stories concerning his death. My grandmother said the family was told he drank himself to death. They said that something ate up his insides. Today we would call it cancer. The other story, which I believe to be true, was that Momma Goldpiece shot him. She caught him molesting her daughter, so she went and got his shotgun and hit him once in the chest. Apparently, he had been molesting her for quite some time and Momma Goldpiece could not ignore it any longer. Supposedly George was a product of this ongoing molestation. Momma Goldpiece's daughter gave birth to George when she was 12 years old. Momma Goldpiece raised George as if she gave birth to him herself. Her pride never superseded the family structure, as criminal and heinous of an act as it was. So many families had been ripped apart by the slave institution that Momma Goldpiece refused to let an illegitimate child break up her family. She carried on with life as if George's existence was as natural as conception and child development could be.

No one spoke publicly about the conception of George. The only thing George knew was that his father was dead, which was true. He never knew that his sister was his biological mother, or that the person he called Mom was actually his grandma. Family secrets remained intact, as Momma Goldpiece vowed to keep her family as close as she possibly could. As life took its toll on her frame over the years, Momma Goldpiece still continued to dedicate her life to the well-being of those who resided inside that ranch home, 55 miles south of Atlanta, Georgia.

CHAPTER 29

IDIOMS: 1973, BIG FISH

An idiom is a phrase or expression whose meaning can't be under-stood from the ordinary meanings of the words in it. You can't extract the definition of the phrase based on the words in the phrase. It has no literal meaning. The artistry in sentence construction allows the power of words to describe emotions, feelings, behavior, under-standing and or intent. And if someone isn't accustomed to decoding certain traditional or cultural idioms, you may have to speak in exact terms. Sometimes the idioms are geographically constructed, and race, age, and or cultural awareness won't allow you to decipher the mean-ing of the expression. I've used Philly slang in idiom form, and I've lost relatives who weren't from the area. At times idioms are used to emphatically express a viewpoint. These phrases add more color to the conversation, as well. And, idioms can offer connectivity and clarity.

I'm not sure if history repeated itself, or if the torch was passed along. Either way, without much complaint, my grandmother became Momma Goldpiece. The setting changed, though. We were no longer in rural Georgia, with dirt roads and chicken farms. I mean, the men-tality and care was present, but the scenery was much grander. It was

1973. It was North Philadelphia. It was bell bottom pants and afro hairstyles. The top R&B songs from 1973 were covered by Marvin Gaye ("Let's Get It On"), Gladys Knight and the Pips ("Neither One Of Us"), Roberta Flack "(Killing Me Softly With His Song"), Aretha Franklin ("Until You Come Back To Me"), Stevie Wonder ("Superstition"), The O'Jays ("Love Train"), and Harold Melvin and The Blue Notes ("The Love I Lost). Kenny Gamble and Leon Huff's creation of the Philadelphia Sound gave the city musical relevance. The Philadelphia 76ers were the historical worst, and the Miami Dolphins were perfect. Roe vs Wade fought for national news headlines with Watergate. And on a cold winter morning in late January 1973, I was born to a 19-year-old girl who lived in the heart of North Philly. Like the character Jerome from the sitcom, "Martin" used to say, "73 was my year."

The '73 version of Momma Goldpiece was slightly different from the original. Annie Grisham Allen revolutionized the position. She was the toughest member of the family and she only stood 5 feet, 6 inches tall. Her weight fluctuated between 160 and 225 pounds. She was a southern caramel complexion—meaning two shades darker than light brown—with thin coarse hair that didn't hold curls for long periods of time. Childhood pictures of her showed resemblance of a cross between African American and Native American. But at the age of 48, and after giving birth to 7 children and raising 30 grandchildren, her youthful beauty had escaped her. Nevertheless, she was as feisty and as proud as they came. It is amazing to me how a sixth-grade dropout became the backbone of an entire family. We embraced her, our street embraced her, the entire neighborhood embraced her. She was mom to the entire community. The rural ranch in Lincoln, Georgia, had turned into a three-story row home on the 2600 block of N. Sixth Street.

The North Philadelphia neighborhood had morphed into a mixture of low-income families of African American and Puerto Rican heritage. On average, there were about three children per household, with 85% of the block being headed by either married or common law couples. The block was composed of 50 row homes—25 on each side of the block. The west side of the block had two-storied homes, and the east side had three-storied homes. Traffic flowed solely in a southerly manner, as cars could park on the west side of the street. The 2600 block of N. Sixth St was intersected by Lehigh Avenue at one end, and Huntingdon Street at the other end. Usually the neighborhood kids loitered at the Huntingdon Street end. A Jewish family owned a convenience store on the northwest corner of the block, and the neighborhood winos owned the northeast corner. The block was overpopulated with kids, and at any given time you could see girls jumping rope or playing hopscotch, while the boys played step-ball and football.

My grandparents' house was closer to Lehigh Avenue. It was on the three-story side of the block. Four steps led to a screenless brown door, with the number 2615 written horizontally across it. My grandfather used his GI Bill to mortgage the house. I always wondered why he chose to purchase a home in a resource stricken, gang infested neighborhood? As a retired veteran, why didn't he use the Bill or other housing stipends to do what his white counterparts did? They moved to new homes, in newly constructed neighborhoods. They sought to improve the quality of life for themselves and their families. Why didn't he do the same thing? My ignorance allowed me to ignore that suburbanization allowed communities to blatantly institute strict housing policies that excluded many families of color.

These communities were socially engineered, and purpose driven. The creation of the middle class was exclusive. Someone decided to move industrial park and textile jobs to the periphery of Philadelphia. Someone said they were going to build a community around the plants—build shopping centers and supermarkets, build new homes, and implement strict criteria for potential applicants. They sat in a room and devised a plan for support and implementation. A plan to guarantee that the best teachers would be recruited, and the preferred race would be serviced. They socially engineered everything so that even high school curriculums would offer classes that encouraged post-industrialized critical thinking. They exposed the preferred to industry that was on the horizon. They constructed a community, distant from public transportation, distant from public consumption, distant from forced racial interaction—in both schools and public space.

An example of this urban reconfiguration took place when Northeast High School moved from its original location. The building was renamed, but the structure didn't possess the same substance as the original entity. Thomas Edison High School would occupy the same space as Northeast High. All of the teenage kids that resided on Sixth Street would be forced to consume inadequate public education, because Northeast High School took its name and resources to the periphery of Philadelphia.

During the Vietnam War, more soldiers died in combat from Thomas Edison High School than any other high school in the country. Of the 58,220 fatalities from the war, 64 of them had attended Thomas Edison High. When Northeast High moved, it took its alumni support, its teachers and its resources. What was left was a shell of educational promise, permeated by drugs, gang violence and the loss of hope. This was human generated; this was intentional. And after peeling back the layers of the political, social, and economic climate of our country, I discovered the ignorance in my own question. I asked my grandfather this question as if he had true control of outcomes and opportunities—as if he had a choice. As chaotic and overcrowded it may have been at times, he was just happy to provide the family with stable shelter. Anything extra would be icing on the cake.

The house on N. Sixth Street had a basement, a living room, a kitchen and five bedrooms. Utility outlets were present. However, payment of those utility bills determined whether they functioned. Sometimes they had electricity and sometimes they didn't. Same thing with the heat—especially after the 400% spike in oil prices caused by the embargo. When the gas was cut off, the 20 people who lived inside 2615 N. Sixth Street used kerosene heaters to warm the house, and "hot-plates" to cook with. The hot plate was used to heat up water for baths, blaze frying pans for fried chicken—and at times, to even warm hands and feet from winter frost.

The house was occupied by my grandparents, Annie and JT, their four daughters, Sheila, Janet, Ann and Evelyn and their young-est son Terry. Their oldest son and daughter, Willie and Sarah, didn't live there, but both of Sarah's daughters did. Evelyn's six children and her boyfriend, Big Freddy, claimed 2615 as their residence as well, as well as Ann's four children. Twenty people lived inside 2615 N. Sixth Street. The house also welcomed a host of visitors on a daily basis. Neighborhood kids, boyfriends, girlfriends, cousins, distant relatives, all made their way in and out of the three-story row home.

Bodies and foot traffic didn't stop my grandmother from ruling with an iron fist, though. She was free flowing except when it came to dishes being left in the sink and furniture not being in order. Instantly, she'd turn into 5-feet-6 inches of thunder if either of her pet-peeves weren't in order. She didn't have a lot, but she took care of what she had. One day she came home and noticed $35 was missing from her bedroom drawer. Man, she came downstairs and raised hell. With a house full of people, it's common for stuff to be used or taken. But everyone knew never to touch her stuff.

So when her money was missing the entire house was held hostage, including the people who didn't live there. As she held court, someone mentioned that my mom's boyfriend had just left the house. My grandmother snatched her purse and house keys off the dining room table with one hand, like she was playing a game of jacks. As she glided across the floor, my cousin Fuzz informed my grandmother that his brother left dishes in the sink. She continued to float towards the door while uttering, "Boy, I ain't thinkin' bout those damn dishes—I got bigger fish to fry." And off she went, running down Sixth Street hoping to catch my mom's boyfriend before he got away. It would be my first introduction to the use of an idiom. But it definitely wouldn't be my last.

CHAPTER 30

IDIOMS: THE WAIT

MARCH 4, 2019.

For the entire four hours and forty-six minutes I sat on that SFO to MIA flight, my mind never left the realm of control. I had mapped out what was going to happen the minute I stepped inside the courthouse, and what time I was going to head back to the airport. I had several return flight options. There was a flight later that evening, or early morning the next day. I said to myself, if I miss shootaround, I'll make sure I email Brad to see what he wants to do about the pregame edit. I had it all figured out. And four hours and forty-six minutes was enough time to think about and construct an efficient game plan. I knew the government was expecting to meet briefly before I took the stand. I didn't think it would be intense, though. Most, if not all of the information I would be asked was already on record. They would just be confirming the statements I made at the grand jury hearing. Nothing new. I had admitted to and plead guilty to said charges several months prior. I didn't deny it: I did it. Plus, it wasn't like they didn't have the proof anyway.

And although I had to formally regurgitate already known information, I took some of the flight time to rehearse. I asked and answered my own questions. I tried to be the prosecution and the defense. I tried to anticipate, I tried to get out in front of potential angles that the defense may try to exploit. I kept saying, "Pooh, what else?" I was trying to be efficient once I landed. No surprises, no hiccups. Walk in, meet, take the stand, answer a couple of questions, and get out of there. Easy as 1, 2, 3. I even huddled up with myself: put both hands in and said ready, break! like it was a team circle dispersing. The plane landed, I walked to the airport restroom, put on my tie, tightened the laces on my Allbirds, tucked my shirt in, pulled up my suit pants, looked in the mirror, checked my teeth for debris, took a deep breath, exhaled and said, "All right Pooh, let's get this over with. You'll be back on the West Coast before you know it."

This was the first time in my life that I would be called as a witness. And for this case, a witness for the government, the prosecution. When I testified at the grand jury hearing, all of the questioning was done by the prosecution. I was informed this setting would be slightly different. Both parties would have opportunities to ask questions. Simple, straightforward, easy. Right? Not exactly. The government had carved out a four-week time slot for this trial. By the time I landed in Miami, they were in week seven. They had asked the courts if my sentencing could trail the trial. And by this point, I was ready to testify, I was ready for trial to be done, I was ready to accept sentencing, I was ready to get on with the rest of my life, I was ready to get back to San Francisco.

Once I arrived at the courthouse, I was escorted to an office area. Small pleasantries were exchanged between myself and two FBI agents, as we walked the maze-like hallways. Prior to pointing out the designated seating area, the FBI agent turned to me and asked, "Is everything squared with your hotel reservation?" I was confused. Maybe he had my obligations mixed up with another witness. The trial had been going on for a while, and I was sure all parties involved were nearing the point of exhaustion.

I said, "Hotel? I wasn't aware that I'd be staying the night. I knew it was a small possibility—has it been determined yet? Are you sure? If they are ready, I'm ready to roll. I don't need a hotel."

The Agent informed me the trial was running longer than expected and that they were hoping to get me on, if not that afternoon, hopefully Tuesday morning. In calculation, I thought to myself, "OK, so if I go on tomorrow morning, and if I'm off the stand before noon, I can grab a flight, land, Uber straight to Oracle Arena and be there by tipoff. That's not bad, one night in a hotel won't kill me."

That afternoon, once the court broke for recess, the Assistant U.S. Attorney thanked me for being flexible—as if I had a choice. The defense was dragging out cross examinations and it was a bit taxing, but they were only doing their job. We talked for a little bit and he informed me that I would not be called that afternoon and that he was hoping they got to me tomorrow morning. It all depended on how the afternoon went. If I didn't get called tomorrow morning, then that meant I would not make it back in time for the game. He told me that I could hang around the office, or leave and go back to the hotel and return to court in the morning. I decided to leave. I had to wait until my phone, taken as I entered the federal building, was returned before I could coordinate with the government's booking agent to retrieve a hotel. I Ubered to the hotel, walked to the registration desk, gave them my confirmation code, took the room key, walked to the elevator, and stared at the signaling button. Frustrated that I was about to ascend into a foreign rest space, I smirked and said to myself, "And you thought you had it all figured out."

Tuesday morning, I checked out of the one-night stay and headed over to the courthouse. I was there by 8 a.m. I was given an update of the previous afternoon's progress. Again, there was a possibility I would be called, but the government wasn't sure. I had packed three pairs of underwear, deodorant, a toothbrush, olive oil and no changing clothes. Same suit, clean underwear, and pearly whites, all accompanied my person on Day Two. The morning passed without me being called to testify. Again, court broke for recess, the Assistant U.S. Attorney walked into the waiting area, gave me an update, apologized for his sense of normalcy and gave me a tiny bit of hope that I might get called in the afternoon.

Reality started to sit in, I would miss our game vs the Warriors. My mother had an NBA League Pass and she didn't miss a Celtics game. I never understood how she could watch the game and the bench at the same time. She would know that I wasn't on the bench for the game, so I started preparing my lie. Outside of my wife, lawyer, and employer, I didn't want anyone to know I was in Miami. My mother would just worry herself to death if she knew where I was. I retrieved my phone again, walked out of the building, called my sister, and told her to tell Mommy I was back in the locker room sick. It was the first of a four-game West Coast swing for us. It was my scout, it was the defending NBA Champs, it was Steph Curry vs Kyrie Irving, it was Kevin Durant vs a young Jayson Tatum, it was Steve Kerr vs Brad Stevens, it was the Golden State Warriors vs the Boston Celtics. I not only had a hand in the preparation, I had a free ticket to watch as well. Instead, my inconsistencies, my failure in character, my wire fraud conviction, would place me in a government witness waiting room, and not at the game.

We won the game that night by 33 points. It would be recorded as the Warriors' worst home loss since Steve Kerr was named Head Coach of the franchise. I watched every second of the TNT broadcast while sitting at the foot of the bed in my hotel room. It's hard for me to enjoy the game as a spectator. Every non-Celtics NBA game I watch, I'm always watching as a coach. Objectives, rotations, angles, pace, spacing—all these things run through my head anytime I watch a basketball game. It's the controlled insanity of a coach. I was really focused watching this game. I had something to say to the television on every possession, on both ends of the floor—as if I was speaking through an intercom system and the players could hear me. The only reason it was painfully agonizing was because we arguably played our best game of the season that night.

Watching the game helped take my mind off the trial. For a quick moment I was lost in my normal responsibilities. I was virtually coaching, I was virtually assisting, I was virtually supporting. After the game the team was busing to Sacramento. The NBA scheduled a back to back to kickoff this 10-day trip. If all went smoothly Wednesday morning, I could catch the team in Sacramento before tip.

Again, I woke up, checked out of the one-night stay, which had now turned into a series of one-night stays, hopped in an Uber and made it to the courthouse by 8 a.m. Same routine, same briefing, same suit, same pearly teeth, but different underwear.

"Jerome, we are getting close, even the Judge is starting to get a little annoyed by the defense. If you're not on by this afternoon, we will start with you tomorrow, for sure."

The DOJ attorney's apologetic posture almost tricked me into believing I was doing them a favor. Before returning to the courtroom, the AUSA dropped a name in my lap. He asked if I ever met the individual or if I knew who he was and what he did for a living. With conviction, I answered no to all his seemingly random questions. He exited the waiting area. I hung around the office, waiting patiently. And again, nothing.

Our Sacramento game wasn't nationally televised, so I knew I wouldn't be able to watch the game live. The hotel informed me they were sold out for the upcoming evening, so I had to change locations. It was nothing for me to up and go because I didn't have any luggage. The next hotel I found was in walking distance of the courthouse so that made my commute a lot easier. I sat in the waiting area until 4:30 p.m. and then I walked back to the Holiday Inn Express on Biscayne Boulevard. Three blocks away was American Airlines Arena. Three blocks away, my life existed in a completely different configuration. Seeing the arena in the backdrop, I started thinking about places and events that my memory attaches itself to in relation to that space.

I thought about the time Aida and I took Roman and Jordyn to game six of the 2013 NBA Finals—the game when Ray Allen back-peddled and knocked down the corner three to tie the game in regulation. We didn't see it live, though. For the entire fourth quarter, 4-year-old Roman was asleep in his mother's arms. In anticipation of wrestling with a large crowd postgame, Aida and I decided to leave the area with three minutes left in the game. We ended up missing the shot. To this day, Jordyn still has the San Antonio Spurs hat she pur-chased that night, hanging on a nail inside her walk-in closet.

It was a nostalgic stroll from Wilkie D. Ferguson Jr. U.S. Courthouse to the Port of Miami Holiday Inn Express. Wednesday night marked the second game in a row I would be absent. The Boston Celtics' patience and understanding throughout all of this was nothing short of amazing. We beat Sacramento that evening, and the team's postgame flight would take them to Los Angeles. The final two games of the trip were scheduled for Saturday and Monday. I didn't feel the added rush to testify anymore. I felt like there was enough time left in the week to take the stand and meet the team before Saturday's game. So I relaxed, but I was still ready to be done.

By Thursday afternoon, with a shortage of clean underwear, I decided to take my frustration out on the pavement. All week, I left court and went straight to my hotel room. No sightseeing, no tanning by the pool, no running on the beach. I wasn't on vacation. But by this time, I either had to order laundry service or purchase new under-wear. I chose the latter. Sarcastically, I kept saying to myself, "Will I get called before my scheduled April 16 sentencing date?" Friday would be the day. I was advised to eat before I arrived. They said it could be a long day, even with the mandated recesses. At this point, I didn't care about having a full stomach—I had bigger fish to fry. We played the Lakers the next night and I was trying to get to LA.

CHAPTER 31

OH REALLY?

Friday morning it was. I was called to the stand, sworn in and seated in front of roughly 50 people, jurors included. The vantage point was strange, though. All eyes were on me—the Judge and the court stenographer were to my left, the jury box was to my right, and the remaining constituents were straight ahead. The prosecution went first. It would be my third time admitting to the said offenses. The first time was at the grand jury hearing when I was indicted. The next time was at my plea hearing. By now, I arrived at trial well versed—more anxious than nervous. It had been a long week. I mean, just getting from Boston to Miami, in itself, was emotionally draining. And to finally arrive in Miami and expect to return to work all in the same day, and it not happen, left me perplexed. One day was cool, two days, I huffed and puffed a little bit. By the third day, all of the jitters passed, and frustration started to set in. Once the fourth day came and went, I felt like I was in a spin cycle.

We went step by step. I didn't speculate, I didn't suggest, I didn't hypothesize. I merely put everything on me. I acknowledged that I too was disappointed in my decisions and my actions. I held myself accountable. There was no one to blame: I could have said no, but I didn't. The prosecution wrapped everything up in 90 minutes. We covered it all and it wasn't even midday yet. The Judge asked the defense how much time they would need. He wanted to gauge how long court would break for recess. The defense didn't give an exact length, so the Judge set our return for 1:15 p.m. And the jury was dismissed first.

Two FBI Agents escorted me into the hallway. As the remaining individuals spilled out into the corridor, one of the Agents asked about the team's lodging location when we play in Los Angeles. It wasn't an odd question because they were aware that the Celtics were scheduled to play the Lakers the next night. They actually were rooting for me. They knew it had been a long week of waiting. They empathized with the unusual work absence required of me to be present in Miami. I told him we go back and forth between Beverly Hills and Downtown. There's a Ritz Carlton Hotel right next to the Staples Center that is convenient and hassle free, in terms of traffic. He said he was familiar with the Ritz Carlton because when they went to LA to conduct their in-person interviews, they stayed at the J.W. Marriott that's connected to the same Ritz. I responded, "Oh really? Cool." And then the Agents took me to the cafeteria so I could purchase lunch.

Court resumed. I took my place on the stand and proceeded to be grilled for the better of three hours by the defense. Three hours. They were slow, meticulous, direct, and intentional. Every word, every question, every gesture. The defense attorney was an expert at both verbal and nonverbal communicative skills. It was as if he'd mastered Webster's Dictionary. He knew which words would cause a juror to sit on the edge of their seat while they waited for my response. He spoke the right language. If I paused before a response, he didn't allow my brain to gather thoughts concerning the open question. He peppered me with additional phrases, in an attempt to fluster me.

In the beginning I kept answering questions by either nodding my head or shaking my head; those movements would constitute a yes or no in court. But the stenographer had no way of recording my nonverbal communication. The defense turned to the jury, looking annoyed, as if he was suggesting to them that I wasn't as sharp as my Ivy League degree would claim me to be. He was the seasoned pro. I was the rookie. It was NBA playoff-like intensity in the room, and I was still in regular season mode. I didn't anticipate his angle. I was a little naïve. I just thought I would get up there and tell the truth, not blame anyone, agree and stay in compliance. I was over the misconception of feeling like a rat. The scars I carried from my childhood had weighed me down to the point where part of me felt guilty for telling the truth. But there was no denying the facts. And The Alphabet shoved them right in front of my face on Day One. I actually thought I was exemplifying the correct behavior by not denying it, by not blaming anyone, by accepting responsibility.

As the clock ticked, and we got deeper into the cross-examination, I started to relax more. It was beginning to turn into more of a conversational joust than one-sided lecturing. There's confidence in the truth. And when you're telling the truth you don't carry any fear. You stand in conviction, in tone and posture. The truth doesn't crack. And in my heart, I really cared about all parties involved, regardless of where we were currently positioned. Three hours passed and the Judge was ready to end both the day and my leg of the trial. The defense informed the Judge that he wasn't finished questioning the witness. The Judge asked how much more time he would need; if it was 15,

30, maybe even 45 minutes, I think we would have proceeded that Friday afternoon. But when the defense said, another hour or two, my whole body almost collapsed. That meant I would miss both the Lakers game Saturday night and the Clippers game on Monday. I was sick. To my surprise, though, the Judge was more than accommodating. He informed the court that we were going to pick up my portion of the trial Tuesday, so that I could get back to work. I almost shouted, "There is a God." The Judge gave the defense and the prosecution final instructions for the day. He dismissed the jury, and then told everyone else to have a good weekend.

I took an 8:30 p.m. flight to LAX that night. The team had been in LA since late Wednesday night following the Sacramento Kings game. We were staying in Beverly Hills at the Beverly Wilshire. By the time I arrived at the hotel, most of the Friday night patronage were already in festive mode. I went to grab my room key from the front desk, but no reservation was coming up under my name. Maybe I was removed because I wasn't present when the team first checked in. I informed the front desk that I was one of the assistant coaches for the Boston Celtics and that if possible, could I use my personal card to secure a room for the evening? Their response was, "Absolutely, but are you sure your travel party is staying here?" I told them I was positive but that I'll call our Head of Security to double-check. I was all over the place. When I inquired with Operations to see if we were staying downtown or in Beverly Hills, I automatically assumed we were staying at the Beverly Wilshire when he said Beverly Hills. Our Head of Security told me I didn't have the correct information, and that we were staying around the corner at the Montage. I laughed and said, "I'm glad it's within walking distance, because I'm cooked." I was happy to be back with the team, on the road, coaching, escaping my reality. I wasn't even bothered by the fact that I would have to take a redeye back to Miami Monday after our Clippers game. The Judge let me travel to LA, he allowed me to rejoin the team. I was tired but elated to be back.

I was all smiles at shootaround the next morning. Both players and staff extended their concerns with my absence. I played it off. The last thing I wanted to be was a distraction. We went on to beat the Lakers that night, and that put us at 3-0, with one game remaining on this West Coast swing. The Lakers/Celtics rivalry is unmatched in all of sports. The atmosphere is different any time the two teams play one another. I was overly excited for this game; not because of my rivalry awareness, but rather because it was my first game back. The only other time in my coaching career I got hype for a Lakers/Celtics game was for Kobe Bryant's last game in TD Garden. Taylor had a sorority event back in Philadelphia, so she couldn't make the game. But Dec. 30, 2015, Aida, Jerome II, Jordyn, and Roman would all be in attendance to watch Kobe play his last game in Boston.

He had 15 points and 11 rebounds that night. The Lakers would secure only their sixth victory of the season in 33 tries. Kobe hit a big 3-pointer late to put the game out of reach. The clock dwindled down to zero and you could hear The Garden fans cheering his name. I hadn't seen him in quite some time, but I decided to walk up to him after several other Celtic players expressed their admiration. He turned around and before I could reintroduce myself, he screams, "Pooooooooooh!" We both smiled and hugged one another. He asked how I have been. I'm not so sure he knew beforehand that I was on the Celtics coaching staff. There was a line of players waiting to greet him on the court, so I told him I'd come in the locker room. I proceeded to turn around and walk off the floor like I always do after a game. Only this time,

I had one hand in my pants pocket, while my other arm swung back and forth hard more—my strut resembled that of George Jefferson during any episode of "The Jeffersons" when he was "feeling" himself. Kobe remembered me. The game had taken him all over the world, and the excitement in his voice when I walked up made me feel like a million bucks.

I took the kids in the locker room to meet Kobe. He was telling them stories about me in my younger days. Can you imagine? Kobe, one of the greatest to ever play the game, sitting there telling your own kids that he stole from their dad's game? It blew my mind. Jerome and Jordyn were in the moment. Roman, however, was not. He was still upset that the Celtics lost the game. So he wasn't up for conversations or photos. It reminded me of the time when Aida and I took Jerome to Game 3 of the Sixers/Lakers 2001 NBA Finals in Philly. Jerome had a poster of Shaq on his bedroom wall. Before jumping in the car to head to the game that day, he ran upstairs to his bedroom and took the poster off the wall. I thought he wanted to show his support for one of his favorite players while rocking his No. 3 Iverson jersey. I really thought his allegiance was split. As soon as we stepped foot inside the Wells Fargo Center, and Jerome heard all of the "Let's Go Sixers" chants, he stopped dead in his tracks, let go of my hand, and ripped the Shaq poster in half. I looked at him, he looked at me and said, "Come on Dad, Let's Go Sixers." Roman had that same fan support in his spirit the day I took him to meet Kobe Bryant. Vanessa and the girls stood patiently waiting in the hallway. As my family and I turned to walk away, Kobe bent over, opened his arms and eloquently said, "Mamacita."

CHAPTER 32

IDIOMS: CLARITY

MONDAY, MARCH 11, 2019.

We had one last game on the trip. Luckily for us, the Lakers and the Clippers play their home games at the same arena. A friend of mine from Philly was going to be in LA, so I offered him my tickets for the Clippers game. I had to take a flight immediately following the game, so I told him I wouldn't be able to hang out afterwards. The team wasn't leaving until the next morning, but I was on a redeye back to Miami. He didn't know why I had separate travel plans, and he didn't ask questions. I planned on taking an Uber right after the game. I asked one of my co-workers if they could take my travel bag back to Boston. Once again, I wanted to travel light to Miami. Our game finished just as my friend from Philly arrived at the arena. His plane from Philadelphia had just landed in LA. I thought he was already in town. I told him I was running up the ramp to catch an Uber, and he said he would drop me off at the airport. It had to be God, because I wouldn't have made my flight if it wasn't for my friend. The wait time for an Uber would have subsequently made me miss my flight. He offered to drop me off at LAX. On the drive, I gave him a brief summary of the ordeal, and he was in disbelief. He pulled up to the airport, we shook hands, I told him I appreciated the ride, and I ran to the TSA line.

Day Two on the stand lasted a little under two hours. The defense brought the closing heat—similar to Mariano Rivera's cutter. His words had a lot of action. They would be the thread-like stitching in the minds of each juror. I wasn't worried about swaying the jury, I just wanted to tell the truth. The entire ordeal had become extremely taxing, both mentally and physically. I was trying to hold cover, but I think had I been on the stand one minute longer, I would have broken down. The travel, the waiting, the questioning, the travel and the questioning again all was piling up. I just wanted to get back to Boston and work on my next scout. At the one hour and 40-minute mark, the defense had asked me if I was aware of six individuals' activities surrounding the case. To each I said I was not aware. The defense attorney asked in a tone that would suggest anything other than the word yes was a lie.

With each calling of a name, the volume increased. The louder he spoke, the more convincing he appeared to be. Most of the names I was familiar with; the activities though, I was not. I remained calm and chose not to engage in the battle of sound systems. I found it to be odd that one of the six names resembled in pronunciation the same name the AUSA asked me about the week before when I was sitting in the waiting room. Before the government mentioned the name, I had never heard of the person. He rested his case, and the prosecution had a chance to re-examine. It lasted all of 30 seconds. After my response he finished by saying, "Your Honor, I have no further questions."

We had reached the end of the day. It was a Tuesday afternoon in southern Florida. This trial was headed into week eight. I was only in court for two days and I was exhausted; I could only imagine how the rest of the court felt. It's not like television, where everything gets wrapped up in a one-hour time slot, actually less than that, if you remove commercial time. The Judge informed the court of their start time for the proceeding day. Immediately following those instructions, the jury was requested to stand so they could exit. Right as they were about to step out of the box, the Judge made them sit back down.

He told them that there was going to be a story in the coming evening's news cycle that was similar to, but not related to the current case and my testimony. He instructed them to not watch or read any articles pertaining to such. He asked if he made himself clear. Every juror was in agreement, and he dismissed them. He thanked me for my time, he wished both me and the Celtics good luck, and then court was adjourned. I took a deep breath, thanked God for seeing me through, and stepped out of the box.

For a brief second, as the elevator in the Wilkie D. Ferguson U.S. Courthouse descended, I felt like I was free. My duties were done. The atmosphere during this ride with the FBI Agents was much more relaxed. When they accompanied me up, the air could have cut me with a knife. But going down, it was different. Smiles, less tension in posture, almost a relief for everyone. I was so at ease that I almost forgot that I had to return in 37 days for my sentencing.

I was facing 21 to 27 months of custodial time. Yet it was the furthest thing from my mind. I was done—no more cross-examination, no more word play. Right before crossing the lobby, we shook hands, and both Agents wished me the best. I stopped by the security desk to recover my phone. I hit the glass doors, took a long inhale of the good Florida air, and headed toward the Holiday Inn Express. American

Airlines had a 9:35 p.m. nonstop flight to Boston, and there was plenty of time before it departed. I kicked around the idea of just staying in Miami for the night to recoup. Take in the good weather, go to Prime 112 on South Beach, and just let my hair down. I hadn't been home in 12 days, though. So I elected to get on at 9:35 flight that night.

As I turned the corner from NE Third Street onto Biscayne Boulevard, my cellphone started to show a ton of message notifications. In the 6 o'clock national news cycle, stories were popping up about a college admissions scandal. I froze in my tracks. I read some of the names that were involved. I started to think about the names that were mentioned when I was on the stand. I thought about the strict orders the Judge gave the jurors before they left the courtroom. And I thought about the FBI agent's comments regarding the in-person interviews they conducted in my case.

Two years before the trial began, I was in that same J.W. Marriott the FBI agent referenced. There, I informed a friend that the FBI showed up at TD Garden. We sat in the lounge of the hotel, sipped coffee, and he casually told me he was aware of their inquiry because they had called him. I didn't think that was how The Alphabet operated. But since I didn't have any proof, I just counted it as me possibly being overly paranoid back then. Now, however, it all started to make sense to me. Unbeknownst to me, my case and conviction ignited a national college admission scandal.

The headlines, the names, the connections were too familiar. I was guilty, I was wrong. I deserved rightful punishment. I deserved the exposure. My integrity didn't match the platform I was afforded. But was I targeted all along? That wasn't the issue now. I had the opportunity to say no and I didn't. This entire ordeal did a tremendous amount of harm to my family and the University.

But after walking out of court, reading all those articles, I called Aida. She answered without even saying hello. She just jumped into mid conversation and said, "Jerome, I'm sitting here watching the local news—oh my God, you are in the middle of some shit."

I responded by saying, "Aida, this is crazy. The Alphabet got bigger fish to fry."

CHAPTER 33

DON'T LOSE WHAT YOU'VE GAINED

When the College Admissions Scandal broke and the Varsity Blues case was compiled, I got called back in. My case, although separate in filing, represented the genesis of the Varsity Blues case. The mental and physical fatigue caused by my 2 ½ year joust with The Alphabet left me empty. I had given it everything, and I was ready to move on with my life. I wasn't oblivious to the fact that I was the recipient of large quantities of grace and mercy, though. But getting the call to come back into the government's office was just excruciating. Once they got you, they got you—so I couldn't tell them I wasn't coming. They were different from the NCAA. The NCAA didn't have jurisdiction to mandate that I be interviewed by their lawyers. And since I wouldn't talk to them, they delivered the stiffest penalty in the history of College Basketball. OK, cool, I'll take it, while knowing that they have college coaches currently coaching who have cheated their entire careers. But since I refused to meet with them, they removed my ability to work in that space ever again. Deservingly so. But I couldn't tell The Alphabet I wasn't going to show up to be interviewed. I didn't have a choice.

Thirty minutes of pouting on the phone to my lawyer didn't change anything. I sat in the car across the street from John Joseph Moakley United States Courthouse in Boston and instantly got in my flesh. They were presenting me with an opportunity: I was going to be asked about the activities of the guys who pointed The Alphabet in my direction in the first place. I was going to have the opportunity to return the favor.

How ironic was this? They sent The Alphabet in my direction and now I'm being asked to share their location. Their fate could possibly be in my hands: their family's sense of normalcy altered, exposure and the personal embarrassment from their failure in character splattered all across the country. I went through it all and now it was their turn. And, I would play a major role in making it happen. Revenge served cold!

But in doing so, I would be losing sight of all that I gained from my exposure. Gaining perspective, identifying hypocrisy, and obtaining relational growth—all would be lost if I walked inside the AUSA's office with the intent of delivering spiteful outcomes. I claimed I was better because of the exposure. I was thankful. Thankful that God showed Himself in ways I had never witnessed before. I grew as a believer, as a husband, as a father, as a friend, as an employee and as a leader. And it took for them to send The Alphabet my way for all of this growth to happen.

Aida would always tell me that sometimes people don't even know when they are being used by God. She would always say, "The actions and words of unaware agents be the things that God uses for our good." In my flesh, I wanted to answer any question the government was about to ask me—whether I knew the answer or not. But after sitting in the car decompressing and praying before I walked into the courthouse, I was able to change my lens. I thought less about me. I started to think about those men and their families. I was thankful He deemed me strong enough to endure. I was thankful that I had Him on my side the entire time—I was praying they did as well.

I sat in the AUSA's office and offered no new commentary. When the interview was done, I walked to the receptionist desk and asked if they validated parking. She looked at me funny. I said, "Parking in downtown Boston is expensive, it doesn't hurt to ask." She sarcastically responded by saying, 25% of her annual salary goes toward parking alone, and that what's left of her government pay barely allows her to keep the heat on in her apartment. I laughed and then told her if we were in another setting, and if we had time, I'd tell her a story about the significance of 25% and the inability to pay utility bills. She referenced her current boredom and said she has nothing but time. I, on the other hand, still carried the spook of being in a Federal Building, so I rejected her offer of listening. She told me she had followed my case and that she was a huge Celtics fan. She wished the team good luck on the rest of the season, and then told me to enjoy the rest of my day.

The blandness of a government office contradicts the high pace of any 60-minute FBI TV series. Storyline, plot, climax, conclusion, all wrapped up in between four commercial breaks makes the couch potato marvel at the speed and efficiency of the government. But in real time, the long hours sometimes require The Alphabet to isolate themselves while they dive into the details. So I felt a little bad because the receptionist was screaming for company, screaming for interaction. Did she really want to know why I get sad every time someone refers to 25 percent? Did she really want to hear my story about an unpaid utility bill? Or was she just tired of sitting in an empty vanilla space, staring at a monitored computer screen?

Jokingly I said, "I'm still under the one-hour parking threshold, so I only have to pay $38. If I make it downstairs in the next 30 seconds, I won't be on the hook for the $54 bucks it cost after the 60-minute mark."

Her next comment would force me to sit down. She said, "If I had to pay a $202,000 fine, I'd run out of here and try and save every penny I could also." I then said, "You want to know why I get sad every time I hear a reference made to one forth, or a quarter or 25%? You want to know what the scar on my left leg has to do with an unpaid utility bill? OK, here's the story."

CHAPTER 34

TWENTY-FIVE PERCENT: A LONG WALK

In 2001 Jill Scott released her single "A Long Walk" off her debut album, "Who is Jill Scott? Words and Sounds, Volume 1." The video for this single was shot from the angle of her walking companion, almost as if the person had a GoPro strapped across their chest. The director's voice does not communicate this specifically but judging by the attire of girls congregating on the front steps of a rowhome, one would think it's a hot summer day in the heart of Norf Philly. The video starts with Jill strolling eastbound down the 2200 block of W. Harold Street. As she reaches the intersection of 22nd and Harold Street, she's greeted by a group of guys hanging out. They exchange pleasantries and one of the common folk on the corner extends a fist bump to the body camera.

The casting agency responsible for filling up the corner placed arguably the best deejay in the history of the craft in this role. It's a quick cameo, but DJ Jazzy Jeff posted on the block like he was from that particular neighborhood. He's from another part of the city, but I'll give him a pass. Again, it's Norf Philly in the summertime and everybody is outside—old heads are barbecuing, and kids are selling water-ice. Jill takes this mysterious person on an unofficial tour of her neighborhood. They are headed to the park, hence, the known destination engulfed by the title track. As she crosses 22nd Street, Murrell Dobbins Tech High School covers the entire backdrop. The current University of South Carolina Head Women's Basketball Coach, Dawn Staley, and the late great Eric "Hank" Gathers once walked the halls of that building. The school's backyard moonlights as the Connie Mack Playground and Recreation Center. It is there that Jill and her companion weave through the playground area and the basketball courts, in hopes of capturing the beauty of both the stroll and the neighborhood.

I've watched this video at least 25 times—not because "A long Walk" is my favorite song, but because the director captured everything beautiful about Norf Philly in the summertime. I've walked to that same playground on numerous occasions. It was a two-block walk from my house. I love Jill Scott for many reasons: for one, her music is awesome; two, she is from Norf Philly; three, she chose to shoot the "A Long Walk" video in our neighborhood; and four, she was my second grade classmate at Thomas M. Peirce Elementary School.

Class pictures from the 1979-80 school year disclose that Mrs. Lewis was our second-grade teacher. Jill's picture divulged a tight bang slightly covering her forehead, while single plaits hung from each side of her head. Each plait was held in place by a ball at one end and a barrette at the other. Her photo occupied the bottom far left corner of the class picture. My headshot could be spotted two rows up on the far righthand side. It revealed my mother's obsession with Vaseline. She had dressed me in my best outfit and splattered more grease on my face than a boxer after he gets cut during a fight. I was shining. There was enough grease on my face to share with the other 29 students in my class.

For the most part, each kid in their respective headshot wore their Sunday's best. That was like an unofficial rule: picture day, you either repeated your Easter outfit or you wore your church gear. The class photo covered an 8"x11" paper stock, with 30 small cubic blocks laid out over five rows. Each block displayed outfits and hairstyles that will cause today's generation to scratch their heads. Each block held spirit-filling memories.

On the bottom row, right next to Jill Scott's photo, a distinctive headshot reminds me why my skin itches every time I hear someone use the words twenty-five percent. My best friend in second grade, Kevin, had his class picture headshot positioned right next to Jill's. Every time I see a photo, or hear his name, my flesh wants to bark out LIFE AIN'T FAIR. Jill's photo makes me proud to be a Norf Philadelphian. Kevin McGaughlin's photo reminds me of what once was—and that one out of four isn't good enough when you're talking about the lives of human beings.

CHAPTER 35

TWENTY-FIVE PERCENT: GUSTINE LAKE

Someone emerged from the back of the office and informed the receptionist that a document was needed. They weren't aware I was in the middle of explanation, so they apologized and extended the receptionist additional time to locate the request. Once they returned to the back of the office, I gestured to abruptly leave, and I apologized for causing confusion. She blew off their request and begged me to continue. I told her I'd hurry up and make my point.

I told her that myself and three of my closest friends used to meet on the basketball court of our junior high school every morning at 7:30 a.m. I told her all four of us participated in the Philadelphia School District Desegregation Program. We each lived in different parts of the city and we caught public transportation to a junior high school that was not our neighborhood school.

Brian lived in a section of Germantown called Brickyard, Kevin lived in Norf Philly, I lived in between the Hollow and Brickyard, and DeAndre lived in East Falls Projects. I told her Kevin and I were close friends from elementary school, but after my mom, sister, and I moved from Norf Philly back to Germantown at the end of my fourth grade year, I lost contact with Kevin. So for us to end up at the same junior high school was somewhat of a small miracle. I told her that by the time I entered seventh grade at Woodrow Wilson Jr. High School in 1984, I had lived in four different places. We lived at 2615 N Sixth St. until I was 2 years old. My grandparents lost that house, so the family had to split up. My mom and I moved to Johnson Home Projects with her oldest sister. My Uncle Dooley used his GI Bill to help my grandparents purchase another house in the Germantown section of Philadelphia. So my mother, father, new sister and I moved into my grandparents' new home.

We stayed at 4601 Germantown Avenue until I was 5 years old. My dad's sister agreed to allow the four of us to move into their home in Norf Philly. I told the receptionist I attended Thomas M. Peirce Elementary school from first to fourth grade, while we lived at 2717 N. Bonsall Street. My parents split up that summer, and consequently my mom, sister, and I moved back to my grandparents' house in Germantown. I told her I finished fifth and sixth grade at John Wister Elementary School. And for middle school I got selected to participate in the District's desegregation program. Supposedly, I was being sent to a "better" school.

Sadly, our family was convinced that schooling in a neighborhood with less color configuration would be an ideal incubator. Hence, at the start of the seventh-grade school year, my 11-year-old self had to take two buses and a train to get to school. This commute was common for many African American students throughout the city. We were being bused to the northeast. It's ironic that the same flight caused by suburbanization, the same socially engineered communities that instituted policies and procedures to exclude certain races, was now requiring inner city kids to populate classrooms.

Brian took the J bus, DeAndre took the R, Kevin took the 54, and I took the 23 trolley. Each bus would allow the four of us to connect with the Broad Street Subway line from four different stops. Brian connected at the Logan Station; DeAndre connected at Hunting Park; and I got on at Erie Avenue. Kevin had the longest train ride; he got on at the North Philadelphia Station. If we were lucky, we all would leave our homes in time to connect with the same train. Even if it didn't line up, we usually would arrive at the Fern Rock Train Station in enough time to be on the Y Bus together. That would ensure that all of us made it to the court in time to play ball before the school bell rang. I told the receptionist that snow and or cold didn't stop us from playing pickup. Rain might have slowed us down, but for the most part, the four of us were married to the court. We were all close in skill and talent, and we pushed one another.

One day DeAndre told us about a basketball league he played in outside of school. He invited the three of us to come and try out for the team. We were hesitant—he was from East Falls Projects. If you weren't from that neighborhood, you just didn't go and randomly walk around by yourself. He assured us we would be fine. Although we were afraid, our love for the game trumped our fear. Plus, DeAndre was a year older than us and he got a lot of respect around school, so we figured he was respected in his neighborhood too.

I paused in the story and asked the receptionist if she wanted me to just spit out the numerical significance. She asked if I could do just that, and then go back to where I left off. So I told her. I said I get upset every time I hear an expression with 25% in it because I was the only one from our group to make it out. I told her that DeAndre was stabbed to death inside a car when he was 17 years old. I told her that Brian died of an overdose when he was 23 years old. I told her that Kevin was a homeless crack addict. Then I told her, "And then there's me."

I told her that DeAndre's invitation changed my entire life. I got over my fear of going to another neighborhood to try out for a basketball team. I told her I went to Gustine Lake Recreation Center with DeAndre that day. And that while in that center, one day I was noticed doing homework in the Director's office. I told her I was only in that office doing homework that one time. All the other times I was in the Director's office, I was trying to steal sodas, ping pong balls, anything I could get my hands on. But the one day when I decided to do homework inside the office, I was spotted by the Director, Bob Johnston. He and Tennis Young took it upon themselves to call James Flint, who then called Dan Dougerty, who then called my mom and asked if she'd be interested in getting me tested for entrance into an independent school.

The next thing I know I'm wearing a blazer and tie to school. I told her the opportunity was presented just like that—it was that random. It seemed like just yesterday, the four of us sat on the back of the Y Bus drinking forties before school. And next I'm traveling in a completely different direction—literally. The Y Bus took us to the Northeast, to a socially engineered failure. The 65 Bus took me to the Main Line, to a suburban utopia. The Y Bus kept me in the familiar. The 65 Bus transported me to a whole new world. Me, Brian, and Kevin went to Gustine Lake Rec Center and all of us tried out for the team. It was DeAndre's neighborhood. But because of a random act, I got the opportunity to go to a private high school. One out of four got an opportunity. Life ain't fair.

Gustine Lake led to Episcopal Academy. And Episcopal Academy led to the University of Pennsylvania. And to think all of it happened because of DeAndre. Brian gave me the money to catch the bus to get to the tryout that day. And to be honest, I only went to the first practice because Kevin said he was definitely going. Yet all their life trajectories look drastically different from mine. How can I not be affected by the numbers? So, one out of four hurts. It's something I've carried with me my entire life.

The receptionist interjected, "So, Mr. Allen, let me ask you a question: if you always carry an element of this supposed survivor's guilt, how then could you manage to commit wire fraud? After hearing some of your story, I'm even more confused as to how you could lose sight of the privilege associated with coaching college basketball— especially at your alma mater. A kid from as you say it, Norf Philly, gets a chance to go to private school, then to The Wharton Business School at The University of Pennsylvania, then goes on to play in the NBA and in Europe, and then comes back to be the Head Coach of the same University he attended—how can he have such a failure in character? I didn't mean to cut you off, Mr. Allen, but after listening to you just now, I couldn't help but to ask these questions."

I looked at her and said, "A mess precedes a message, just like a test precedes a testimony. And the aggregate of my brokenness and contradictions only points to God's grace and mercy."

She looked at me and smiled. "Well, what about the unpaid utility bill story?"

I chuckled and began to tell it.

I was 17 years old and couldn't talk on the phone after 9 p.m. My mom wasn't a strict parent, but she wasn't lenient either. She was in the middle, if that makes sense. She parented my sister and I out of paranoid love. She was well aware of the elements engulfing our neighborhood and could not allow her hovering guard to be relinquished at any time. So, when her son, who stood six-foot-three his junior year of high school, wanted to engage in conversation with his girlfriend via telephone, he had to make sure all dialogue was wrapped up by 9 p.m. sharp. There was no getting around the time frame, either. You see, we had a "one-way." Although our push-button phone connected to the wall via a 50-foot cord, it only allowed for one conversation at a time. No call waiting: you would get a busy signal if you tried to call the phone line that was in use. Even if my mom wasn't home at night, if she called the house after 9 p.m. and didn't get through, she would know that I was on the phone. Plus, she had an in-house enforcer, as my sister lived for any opportunity to get me in trouble.

My grandparent's house had three different phone lines. Three different lines meant three different bills. Three different bills meant three different names. There was a line for the entire house, dominated primarily by my grandma and my aunt. My mom's line was connected to the second-floor front bedroom. And my aunt Sheila had a line on the third floor. This may sound strange nowadays because everyone has a personal cellphone. But back in 1990, all of us communicated via house phone.

The second-floor front bedroom was shared by my mom, sister and I. Resemblance of the bunkbeds my sister and I used to have remained by that time in the form of one twin size frame and mattress.

The other side of the room possessed a full-size box spring and mattress. My mom and sister shared the full-size bed and I slept on the twin.

One night, while my mom was out with her boyfriend, I decided to breathe through the receiver and monopolize the phone. For almost two hours I sat on the phone and talked to my girlfriend about absolutely nothing. We asked one another what the other person was doing at least 20 times. We would breathe, and then sit in dead silence for 30 seconds to a minute, repeatedly. That's what we used to do. We asked questions we already knew the answer to: questions like, What time are you waking up in the morning? What bus are you going to catch in the morning? What are you going to wear tomorrow?" We rested in the fact that we actually communicated. Most of the time about nothing meaningful, but at least we picked up the phone.

At about the 90-minute mark, my sister blurted out that she wanted me to get my water off the hot plate. It was getting late and she wanted to take her bath. I immediately covered the phone with both of my hands because I didn't want my girlfriend to know we didn't have running hot water in the house. I wanted to kill my sister for announcing our hardships out loud. There was a one-eye hot plate plugged into the wall socket of our bedroom and we placed a pot onto it to heat up water. After the water reached boiling temperature, we then poured it into a basin and walked the basin down the hallway to the bathroom. We dumped the boiling water into the tub and mixed it with running cold water. The hotter the water from the hot plate, the higher the water level would reach in the tub. If I was lucky, I'd get a chance to take a bath in roughly 2 inches of water. That's not the exact measurement, but you get my point. No hot water because our gas was cut off? No problem. Get a hot plate, get a pot, fill it with cold water, and then heat it up. That was our routine.

It was getting late and my sister was ready to take her bath before going to bed. There was one problem, though – I'd filled up the pot that was currently on the hot plate, so she had to wait. I could have allowed her to use the water, since I wasn't ready. But that would have made too much sense, and I thought my sole existence in the world was to make her life miserable—or at least that's what I thought her connective purpose was in my own life. So I was being petty. The hot plate was strategically placed far away from anything flammable in the room. It sat near the entrance to our room, roughly 15 feet away from the full-size bed. I laid horizontally across my mom and sister's bed, talking to my girlfriend.

Being six-foot- three meant both of my feet dangled off the end of the bed. Thirty minutes after covering up the phone, I finally agreed to hang up. When I pushed up from the bed and stepped down onto the floor, guess what my left foot stepped into? A pot of boiling water. My sister got tired of waiting for me to finish my conversation, so she removed the pot from the hot plate and placed it right underneath my dangling foot. From the bottom of my left calf to the tip of my big toe, my skin melted like a Snickers Bar left on Las Vegas Boulevard during the month of July. It was the worst pain I had ever felt in my life. I was screaming, but the shock from the image kept me silent. I was crying but no tears flowed down my cheeks. They called my mom and her and her boyfriend rushed me to the emergency room.

The combination of the pain and the gauze sticking to my flesh prohibited me from going to school the next day. When I finally did return to school two days later, I was asked how I burned my foot. I told the people at school that my sister accidently bumped into me while I was making a cup of tea. I told them I had a slight cold and a bad cough, so I thought hot tea would help. I even started to fake a cough in front of them. I would have told my girlfriend the truth before I told anyone the truth at Episcopal Academy. I was already looked at as being the poor city kid.

That morning, I boarded public transportation on crutches, as bandages outfitted my lower left leg. Most of the high school students at Episcopal Academy either drove themselves to school, or nannies or parents dropped them off. They had blazers and clean dress shirts. I had stolen sweaters from Sears. I could never tell anyone at school we didn't have hot water in the house.

With a smile on my face, I wrapped up the story by telling the receptionist, "So I got my left foot deep-fried because of an unpaid utility bill."

She looked like she wanted to convey a tiny aggregate of sympathy. But my smile fractured the seriousness. And it allowed her to ask me one final question.

She said, "Mr. Allen, can you tell me what the hot plate story has to do with the significance of twenty-five percent?"

"Nothing. Nothing at all. It does allow me, though, to segue into answering your original question. Each story is just part of my story - the twenty-five percent reference, the hot plate, and my recent failure in character —the wire fraud conviction—are all just parts of my story. No single event or experience stands as the sole representative of my story. I am the summation of all of my experiences. Romans 8:28 says, 'And we know that in all things God works for the good of those who love him, who have been called according to his purpose.' It doesn't say some things, it doesn't say only good things - it says, 'in all things.' Therefore, good and bad are connected and essential."

Did I call on God when I needed Him? Yes. Was it our first-time meeting? No. Do I exemplify relational Christian characteristics in every setting, in every decision? I wish I could answer yes to that question. My former college roommate told me someone came up to him last year and asked him when did I start talking about God? He was referencing what so many do when they are in a crisis moment in their life. We all do it—we lean in a little more when life challenges us.

And I'll admit, when The Alphabet established their presence, I called on God with more persistence. I wish I could say that in every setting, throughout my life, I walked with no discrepancy as to who was at the center of my life. But I can't. I wish my former roommate didn't have to defend what he's known to be true over our 28-year relationship. I wish I always walked around bearing evidence of the foundation my father established when I was 6 years old. That I always walked around with that "church every Sunday" glow. That I walked around with the awareness that I could potentially represent the only encounter with Christianity someone may witness. I can't change the past. I can only be more connected to my witness going forward. You see, Excellence isn't linear—Growth is.

ALL THE PARTS

Not everything that is faced can be changed;
but nothing can be changed until it is faced
JAMES BALDWIN

CHAPTER 36

UNDERSTANDING THE WHY: ONE AND DONE

One of my biggest character flaws is that I will try and help even when I'm not in position to help. For some reason my default has always been to give and then figure it out later. That's not responsible—no matter how much I try and camouflage it with nobility. I hide behind this shared collaboration notion, presenting the household I grew up in as the reason why I desire to share as much as I can with whoever's lacking. Growing up, if my aunts didn't share their Food Stamps then sometimes my sister and I would not have eaten. We would have gone to bed hungry. And I watched my mother withhold from herself only to make sure we had. Both her and my grandmother cleaned toilets, made beds, and mopped floors to provide what little they could for our household. These things not only sadden me, they also shape the disposition I own today.

My sentencing judge, my wife and my oldest son all pronounced that, financially, I've never been in the position to help as many people as I've tried to help. I was chastised by all three of them because they couldn't understand why I didn't go about servicing the community in a more economically savvy way. Why didn't I create a 501C-3 and hold charity events to raise funds? I graduated from Wharton but none of what I was doing made business sense. Why would I just do? Why would I fly 36 kids from North Philly to Italy over the course of two summers, without having the proper financial structure in place? Why did I feel compelled to save every kid in the hood? Why did I pay—out of my own pocket—the salaries of the summer job program participants? Why did I always have to identify with the less fortunate? Why couldn't I understand that if I don't take care of myself, I'll never be able to take care of them? Was it something about my ego, my pride or my unaddressed trauma that wouldn't allow me to see that my efforts were wrong?

After reading about all the work I did in the community, and after reading some of the character reference letters, the Judge disclosed at sentencing that I committed wire fraud because I needed the money. She told me that financially, I was all over the place. She said that if I had been a better money manager and more responsible, I would not have been enticed to take money from a parent. So, because I leveraged my position as the Head Coach of Men's Basketball at the University of Pennsylvania to solicit funds from a caring parent, I deserved the forthcoming punishment. She said I employed my awareness of loopholes in the University's admissions process and took advantage of the people who trusted that I'd run the basketball program with integrity. She said I cheated a deserving applicant out of an admissions slot, and that greed and selfishness should be, and will be highlighted.

I heard every word she said. But I wasn't listening. I impatiently endured her soliloquy only to arrive at an opportunity to offer rebuttal. As crazy as this sounds— I got mad. I lost sight of the present significance of where I was. I didn't listen to understand. I listened only to respond. Her words, although seemingly accurate in calculation, made me feel like a criminal. Even at sentencing I was blinded. Grateful, but blinded. I admitted I fractured the University's trust, and I admitted I was wrong in accepting the money. But my posture still held on to a hint of justification.

After the Judge spoke her last words, I stood up from my chair to offer commentary. How arrogant of me. Not that I wanted to have the last word, but I wanted and needed to tell the Judge that I didn't do it because I needed the money. That wasn't it at all. My wife, my son, my sister, my best friend and my favorite Penn parent, were all screaming for me to sit my dumb ass down. I even saw Ron, my lawyer, bow his head, as if to say, "Idiot, just shut the fuck up."

"Well, Mr. Allen, why then did you do it?"

As a coaching staff, we always stood on the "40 Year" foundation. Penn didn't offer athletic scholarships, so we were in the business of convincing parents that the financial investment required for their child to attend an Ivy League university would return significant dividends in the future. It's a 40-year decision and not a 4-year decision. We told parents that Penn and its 300,000 living alumni would help their student/athlete reach unimaginable academic and career heights.

I would encourage parents to comb through the University's database, or to just simply Google search what Penn graduates were doing in the world today. Whatever career aspirations they had, we as a basketball program had the ability to connect them. We had to sell the school and its potential as it pertained to the student athlete's bottom line. I would always state with conviction that people cared about Penn and Penn Athletics. So if it's business, medicine, technology, law, politics, consulting—anything they could think of—we as a coaching staff had the ability to connect our players to it.

It wasn't a company line. It was the truth. I always saved my own story as a student athlete for this part of the conversation with parents. I would tell them about the internships I had when I was an undergrad at the University. I'd also bring to their attention that I had four job offers after I retired from playing professional basketball: three in the financial services field, and one in education. All through Penn connections. I would tell parents my high school recruiting story and inform them that our nonconference game schedule would be one of the toughest in the country. I promised the families we would play against Duke and Kentucky. I packaged it all together: come to Penn and experience all that college has to offer, both academically and athletically.

That was what I was selling. I sold my own story, my own experience, in hopes of getting parents to understand that whatever cost was asked of them would be a justified trade-off so their son could get a great job after graduation. That was my competitive advantage anytime I was competing against an athletic scholarship decision. Come to Penn and I'll connect you to the world. I not only played at Penn, I am now the Head Coach of the Athletic Department's flagship program. And there isn't an alum I can't get on the phone with for your son.

If the family's financial aid read demanded the expenditure of $40,000 over four years, it was worth it. Full tuition over an 8-semester life cost a family close to $240,000. Some parents got it right away. Others needed more convincing. Some recruits and their parents understood what attending an Ivy League school meant. Others were completely in the dark. Some families needed close to full financial aid support. Some qualified for considerable relief. Some had to and were willing to pay the full boat. Generally speaking, if your family household income was $60,000 or less, you went to Penn for free. If it fell between $70,000 and $250,000, you could potentially be asked to pay 10% of the family's combined household income. The final suggested request fluctuated, depending on the number of siblings living in the house and concrete debt to asset holdings. Anyone recording combined earnings above $300,000 rarely qualified for aid.

Many of the student/athletes that I recruited who came from affluent families quit the team after their freshman year. They knew how difficult it was to get accepted to an Ivy. They were fully aware of the significance of the setting. And although they were good high school basketball players, they weren't blinded by hoop dream aspirations. So they used the recruiting process. I'd say roughly 80% of the student athletes who came from access quit the team after their freshman year.

It didn't matter whether we as coaches were depending on them to fill out our team's roster or not. They got into school and that was their main objective. Without the ability to dangle an athletic scholarship over their heads, I was left to deal with whatever decision they made. Their status as an undergrad wasn't contingent upon their position on the basketball team. Once they matriculated as an undergrad, they were free to do whatever they wanted to do on campus.

By year three, this phenomenon was starting to eat at me. It almost changed our entire recruiting model as a coaching staff. I wanted to say, "I wasn't recruiting any more rich kids." But in the back of my mind I knew I couldn't afford to limit our talent pool. Plus, one of my college teammates came from an affluent family and he was a beast. He was an integral part of three Ivy League Championship teams. I couldn't completely shut the door on that demographic. And then it happened again. So I developed a disdain for the privileged.

CHAPTER 37

UNDERSTANDING THE WHY: INTERNSHIPS

B eing the head coach, I would get calls all the time from people seeking help with the admissions process. The request came from non-student athlete families as well. One day I got a call from an alum asking me if I could reach out to Admissions. A friend of his had a child who applied to the University and was put on the deferred list. They wanted to know if I'd be willing to speak to Admissions on the student's behalf. In return, the family would support the Basketball Program in fundraising efforts and summer jobs.

This was important to me. Most people thought the University funded the Basketball Program outright. But both the Men's and Women's Head Coach were obligated to foster relationships and help raise money for the programs. Now, I'm not saying I was the reason this particular student ultimately got into the University, but I did call "up campus."

I remember during my twins' application process, Admissions gave no premature indication of acceptance. I had a good feeling the two of them were going to get into school. But the Admissions Office never released early communication on a decision. I had to wait, and my kids had to check their portals just like every other Early Decision Applicant. Ultimately, the deferred student matriculated that coming fall.

The following spring semester, I called the same parent to see if they would help one of our current players obtain a summer internship. The parent was in the position to make it happen but elected to look at our student athlete as a regular applicant. I was informed that all the internships had been filled. And consequently, they were sorry they couldn't help.

I lost it. I was so mad I started foaming from the mouth. Here it was that I had an African American kid who didn't come from access, who was depending on me to be the bridge to exposure and opportunity, and I didn't come through. I sat in his parents' living room two years prior during the recruiting process and told them to their faces that I would receive the baton in their son's maturation marathon. I told the family I'd exhaust myself and not allow their son to go through college in a basketball bubble. I was aware of his "probably not going to happen, but I hope that it happens" dreams. And as much as I tried to push our players to be their best on the court, most, if not all of them would go on to be professionals in something other than basketball.

So many African Americans clutched the elusive dream of professional sports, and I was fighting to change that narrative. In my mind, that's what I was going to do as a college basketball coach. I thought about the transformative African American college basketball coaches who impacted the landscape. I was charged by John Chaney, John Thompson, and Nolan Richardson. Since its inception in 1955,

I was only the third African American to lead a Philadelphia Big Five Men's Basketball program. I couldn't just win basketball games. I had to have impact.

To not be able to secure this internship for this young man forced me to ask myself Why did I help the alum in the first place? And because of this rejection, I said I'd never help again, unless they displayed the capability to help the program. I convinced myself the help was for the players. But it wasn't until my sentencing that I realized the help was about me all along. Aida had once told me all of my attempts to help inner city kids wasn't of God. She told me it was all my ego and my desires. I got defensive, much like I did at sentencing. I kept saying, I was wrong for accepting the money, but I didn't do it for the money. I got angry because they couldn't see what I was seeing.

I'd talked myself into believing that the 2008 Honda Fit I drove was proof I didn't do it for the money. Or the fact that Aida and I still lived in the same house we purchased in 1998 stood as evidence I didn't do it for the money. I even pointed to the trumped-up $300,000 tagged on my case as validation that I didn't do it for the money. I created a narrative in my mind because I knew the government and the media needed to legitimize a figure that would deliver a shock. I was in court, facing 27 months of custodial time. God had showered me with grace and mercy, and here I stood before the Judge—defiant in posture, prideful in attitude, only worried about making sure I proved that I didn't do it for the money. Even at sentencing, the elements of exposure were revealing I was still a work in progress.

CHAPTER 38

ACCESS AND PRIVILEGE: THE REFRIGERATOR

The Judge saw that I was needy. I wanted to argue that others were needy. That's how I wanted everyone to see it. I'm cool. I'm a giver. I have a good heart. I'm not a cup, I'm a funnel. My blessings pass through me. From the NAHA tutoring program to college campus visits, I matched God blessing for blessing. I was clutching the need to be heroic, the need to be a servant leader. Mentally, that adoption would keep my posture mirroring 6 o'clock—straight up and down. I was guilty of said criminal charges, but so was Robin Hood. I've always been willing to leverage what I possessed to support others. It was done for me, so I was returning the favor. I had a strange relationship with access and privilege and my criminal case helped me discover the complexities. It crept into my soul the day the high school I was fortunate enough to attend rejected my younger sister's application.

I matriculated into Episcopal Academy as a freshman in the fall of 1987. Two years later, my cousin Sam was also admitted into the same school. When my mother attempted to register my sister the following year, she was informed of the verdict. Their decision forced me to stand in the tension of feeling lucky because the school changed my life and knowing others would never get the same opportunities. The rejection of my sister's application generated some internal friction that at times has forced me to deviate from solid character traits.

Without Episcopal Academy, my life would have been an empty shell of unrealized potential. The access, the privilege, the exposure I was provided changed the trajectory of an entire family. But a small piece of me carried resentment because the school didn't admit my sister. Being grateful and bitter at the same time is an awkward feeling. My gratitude pushed me to want to provide access and privilege to my own children. But my bitterness fueled the rage that stemmed from the inequalities in the two worlds I occupied. Sam and I experienced a whole new world, both academically and socially. But my sister was left to navigate the spaces of Philadelphia public high schools. I was an athlete. Sam was an athlete. My sister was just a student.

So my disdain for access and privilege probably was conceived when the non-athlete in my own family wasn't granted an opportunity for a better education. I never stopped to consider whether her test scores were high enough to be admitted to an independent school. Or whether Episcopal's allotment of financial aid ran its course. Sam and I required a financial aid package that covered tuition, books, and miscellaneous fees. Maybe the school had a 2-student per house policy or something. I just stubbornly blamed the rejection on her inability to excel on the athletic field. What if it was me? Again, Episcopal Academy changed my life and I was desperately wishing all who came from the same socioeconomic background as I could experience what it had to offer. Especially my sister.

My exposure to access and privilege was a complete contrast to my home life. At home we were appreciative for bare essentials—you know, milk for the cereal, and hot water for baths. I didn't know we were lacking so much until I landed on Episcopal's campus. That's the negative with exposure to new experiences. You never know what you're lacking until you step outside your sense of normalcy. I initially walked the halls of school with my head down. I thought I was seen as the sports jock, the charity case. But I eventually began to embrace my story. I stopped worrying about what others thought of me. I stopped trying to fit in because I never would. I just started being me. I stopped feeling like being broke was a birth curse. The more I excelled on the field, the less inferior I felt. I guess the power of sports allows you to transfer confidence from one space to another. And then, I started getting invited to parties.

Most of Episcopal's student body lived on the Main Line—mansions, grass, driveways, and pools. The house parties I went to in my neighborhood were held in dimly lit basements, with one way in and one way out. On the Main Line, we partied in space and we didn't have to worry about finding the closest exit in case a fight broke out. I had new friends. And I stopped acting like access and privilege was a bad thing. I started to have aspirations of hopefully providing that life to my own children one day.

I used to be mad because the kids at Episcopal had "stuff." I remember going to my first sleepover. It was after a Friday night JV basketball game. The house was spacious, quiet, and comfortable. I slept in a room by myself. By myself. Every room I stepped foot in at my grandmother's house had someone in it. Even if I tried to sleep downstairs on the couch, I'd have to share it with someone. But sleeping in a room by myself and having my own bed gave me a sense of relaxation like you couldn't imagine.

When I woke up the next morning I just laid there and smiled to myself, drowning in the white sheets and fluffy comforter. My teammate walked in the room to notify me that his parents weren't going to cook breakfast. He told me to go in the kitchen, open the refrigerator and help myself. With the comforter wrapped around me like a hotel robe, I walked down the hardwood stairs. Once I got to the kitchen, I saw a huge double door, stainless steel refrigerator tucked 6 feet behind a granite island countertop. The room looked like a kitchen out of the movies. I opened the refrigerator and was overwhelmed by the options. Even today, I catch myself opening my own fridge some mornings and staring at its contents. My body experiences a rush that ends up shifting any perspective that previously stood opposite of grateful. For the grit and perseverance I inherited by watching the effort it took to place a single item inside my grandmother's fridge, I was grateful. But after sleeping in my own room in suburbia for a night, and then waking up to a refrigerator full of food, I was determined to possess ownership of access and privilege.

CHAPTER 39

ACCESS AND PRIVILEGE: SINS OF THE HEART

On the Uber ride from the Wilkie D. Ferguson US Courthouse to the Fontainebleau Hotel, I played it all back. Aida sat as close to me as she possibly could without sitting on my lap—her head on a slight tilt, resting on my shoulder. Neither one of us said a word. Her eyes were closed, and mine were fixated on the moving targets outside the car window. My thoughts were in slow motion. Quietly, I asked myself how did we get here? I jogged my memory—it first landed on introduction. I gave it a second spin and it went further back than that. In doing so, I was able to locate the genesis.

My giving spirit covered elements of envy and jealousy. The drippings of access and privilege fell all around me, yet I never felt like a significant amount fell on me. I knew that comparison was the thief of joy. But I never self-reflected long enough to resist comparison myself. Thinking about applicants from affluent families, I would tell myself, "Those kids don't need Penn, they are set for life." I focused solely on their buying power. I never stopped to think about the educational enrichment all parents desire for their children, regardless of their economic status. Even my own kids get it when they are amongst friends who are less fortunate than them. They are reminded that school and work effort isn't as critical because their dad is "rich." Even if I was rich, and I am not, I'd still push my children to be lifelong learners, to adopt the disposition of forever being in a state of becoming. The judgement, the envy, was relative. My kids were gifted sufficient amounts of access and privilege. But my lens shifted whenever I observed or talked to someone else who manifested it. I was not only hypocritical; I was missing the mark on standards I set for myself.

I stated that my own kids were spoiled, privileged, and entitled. I confessed to playing a huge role in their temperaments. I admitted that I'd made sure their childhoods were different from mine. I justified giving in excess because I never received from my dad. I'd say and admit these things while simultaneously holding onto anger. And if those who came from excessive amounts of access and privilege wanted to be students at one of the top universities in the world, I'd say, "For what? They don't need this intellectual incubator."

But wasn't I attempting to do the same? Why then did I carry vexation, while promoting the same concept? It had to be envy. It had to be jealousy. It had to be the internal hate I felt towards myself for not always making the best business decisions. It had to be the personal shame I wore for not successfully navigating financial terrains so that my immediate family could have generational runs of large-scale access and privilege. I'd been around it. I'd seen it, I'd even tasted it. But I didn't own it. I didn't possess it in order to pass it on to my kids.

I gave, sometimes seeking a hero's acknowledgement. I gave sometimes so that others wouldn't think I forgot where I came from. I also gave because I wanted to offer access and privilege. And by giving an admissions slot to access and privilege, I lost significant portions of access and privilege. We usually gain by giving when it's not transactional. But the privileges I worked my entire life to obtain, vanished in thin air the day I took that bag of cash.

This exposure, my criminal case, has revealed many things. I let go, then reclaimed my faith. I judged, then received judgement. I led with a complaining why. I mistook reputation for integrity. I saw the theme of exposure carry significance throughout my entire life. I was present with no presence in my marriage. And I got to know God in a deeper way. I could reference so much more that found its way to the surface. But none has had a greater impact on me than realizing that there's nothing worse than having a jealous heart.

Having one cost me a lot. It cost me my freedom. It tarnished my legacy. It evaporated my credibility. And it almost silenced my witness. Sins of the heart always pierce the flesh that houses it. Sins of the heart blind you to life's gifts. I chased access and privilege with no awareness that it's relative, subjective and fleeting. I frowned when it was exercised in front of me. I smiled when I was the beneficiary of it. And sometimes I gave it to people from different walks of life.

Coming to the realization that the ownership I sought would never fulfill me was life changing. The essence of the access and privilege I was chasing was represented in the wrong form. I finally realized I had ownership of the right form of access and privilege all along. As a matter of fact, we all do. I just chose to view its meaning from a worldly perspective. And that's where I went wrong.

The access and privilege afforded to us have nothing to do with our works. There's no room to claim ownership based upon our titles or our labor. God gifted it to all of us. Being in alignment and having true understanding of that would have allowed me to avoid sins of the heart. When you journey through life ultimately seeking no other exclusivity, then the root of your imperfections can be better managed. My jealous heart brought to the forefront that having the access and privilege associated with a relationship with God should be my ultimate priority.

I justified my disdain for individuals that came from certain socio-economic backgrounds. But yet I aspired to give the same luxuries to my own family. We all live with contradictions. Even the mirror we stand in front of gives off the opposite of what is. I actually played the hero and the villain in my own story. But now, as I stand on this side of the storm, still broken and still imperfect, I can honestly say I'm a better husband, a better father, a better coach, and a better citizen of the world. The correction offered by The Alphabet allowed me to address the internal turmoil that was driving my decision-making. As painful and embarrassing as it was to my family, to the University, and to all the communities I was connected to, I'm thankful The Alphabet came. For without this exposure, I don't get a chance to move one step closer to being what God designed me to be.

I both wrote my story and personally viewed the story from three different vantage points. Playing the role of victim, hero and villain isn't easy. But by providing context while holding the pen as each distinctive person, I could better create conversations around the theme of contradictions—which ultimately led to me identifying the sins of my own heart. It's enough in this story to strike debate. There are some gray areas that will be populated on both sides. And I'm perfectly fine with that. I found my truth and that's all that matters to me.

There are certain questions I don't answer, and I think that's OK. Maybe by not answering all the questions, you'll agree with me when I say I'm still a work in progress. Even by identifying that my federal case, my outward problem was rooted in internal turmoil, I hope you don't think because of that realization my entire life is now fixed. I've identified what drove me to commit wire fraud, but that doesn't mean all is well. It just means I can now address the cognitive process driving certain actions. Or it could possibly mean the exposure corrected one character flaw, so that I can move onto the next one.

Like, I still have a weird relationship with my dad. And even after witnessing four generations of women in my family shoulder the weight of the structure, I still don't quite mirror the presence in my marriage that Aida deserves. And although I complain less, I still ask God why sometimes. Like why would someone gun down an unarmed jogger? Or why would someone bury their knee into the neck of a defenseless human being?

I've consumed the messages offered by this exposure. God had a unique way of showing me myself. Servitude, kindness, and generosity were all mixed in the pot with hypocrisy, envy and jealousy. Fire boiled all of the ingredients and the dense matter from the bottom of the pot found its way to the surface. God, the master chef, stirred the pot in such a way that all of the isolated products complemented one another.

One day my grandmother offered me plain okra on a plate. I took one bite and almost threw up. Later on that night she put the same batch of okra in a pot and mixed it with some rice, corn and tomato paste. She stood over the stove, added some pepper and a little salt, and then stirred while it simmered. She signaled for me to sit down and try some of her soup.

After my third bowl of okra soup, I said, "Grandmom, you are the best cook in the world. What's in this soup?"

I'm so glad that all of the ingredients housed in my body are being stirred by God the Master Chef. I just gotta get out of His way and let Him stir the pot.

AFTERWORD

Our last regular season game of the 2018-19 NBA season was played at the Verizon Center in Washington, DC. Kyrie Irving didn't make the road trip with the team. He was rehabbing a sore knee. Once he was ruled out for the game, I got excited because I figured I would have an opportunity to attend the NBA Chapel Service held during pregame. For the better of three seasons, I tried not to miss a chapel at home or on the road. But entering my fourth season in the NBA, my pregame shooting assignment required that I be available at the 60-minute mark.

That was Kyrie's slotted shooting time. Each player usually gets 15 minutes of on-court shooting time before every NBA game. With 15 guys on a roster, the times are staggered, starting at 2 and ½ hours before tip, and ending at the 45-minute mark. I was assigned to rebound for three players that season. Terry Rozier loved going at the 105 mark. Marcus Morris went at 75 on the clock, and Kyrie shot at 60. With this being his preferred shooting time, I couldn't make chapel service. About halfway through the season, Kyrie changed his routine. He started doing his pregame shooting immediately following the team's morning shootarounds on the road.

Hence, I was able to attend chapel again. So walking into the Verizon Center, I got excited because I was going to have a chance to hear one of my favorite NBA chaplains. There was one problem, however. Unbeknownst to me, Terry Rozier switched his shooting time for that last regular season game. He elected to take the 60-minute slot. I was a little dejected because I really wanted to talk to Pastor Keith

Battle that evening. But my duties as an NBA assistant coach come first, so I chalked it up.

Pastor Battle taught in those sessions. He broke the Word down —- I'm talking white boards, illustrations, note pads and writing instruments for the players. Every chapel he headed, he treated like a classroom setting. And I appreciated that about him. He gave us access, he extended his contact information to us, as if we were part of the church congregation he shepherds over. I personally experienced that access because I reached out to him several times, and he responded. He followed my case from a distance, and from time to time he sent words of encouragement. Reverend Bob Gray is the Celtics Team Chaplain. He's done a fabulous job of making daily deposits in my life and in the lives of all the NBA players he's come in contact with over his 20 plus years of service. But Keith Battle was my guy. His approach, his style, his transparency, just resonated with me. So when Terry took the time slot, I was a little deflated.

The clock reached the 60-minute mark and Terry and I began our pregame routine. At certain points of the season, I think it's important for coaches to listen to the players. By this juncture, I would ask him how he was feeling. Was it about reps and technique? Was he trying to get a rhythm, or was it about application and carry-over, stemming from our previous postgame film session? The conversation could go in several different directions. Terry said he wanted to make this session about balance, form and rhythm. So off we went. At the 51-minute mark, he looked at me and said he was good. He got out of the session what he was trying to accomplish.

The one thing I learned about this level is that it's important to include players in their own process. I obliged and said, "Cool."

I looked up at the game clock and saw that I had six minutes before chapel ended, and I sprinted off the court. As I turned the corner into the hallway, Tony Dobbins said, "Pooh, Keith Battle came to the locker room looking for you." Somewhat out of breath, as I flew by him I said, "Thanks, Tone." I slid into the locker room door because my old knees couldn't perfect an abrupt stop. Trying to silence my heavy breathing, as I walked into the room, I noticed Pastor Battle was sitting in a locker stall. When I looked at the center of the circle to see who was leading the service, I couldn't believe my eyes.

What's funny is that the voice preceded the presence, and the closer I got to the room, the more distinct the voice got. The more distinct the voice got, the more I was convinced Pastor Battle was using some type of audio device for his illustration. But that wasn't the case. Standing in the center of the room, leading the Washington Wizards chapel that night was Bishop T.D. Jakes. Aida and I were just talking about his new book, Crushing. She was telling me about his app and how she's been able to fill out her week with sermons from our home church pastor, Reverend Dr. Alyn E. Waller and Bishop Jakes.

I took a seat off to the side and listened to him sew into the room. Chapel concluded and I remained in the room until all the players left. I had a specific request for Pastor Battle. He knew about my ordeal and I was one week away from a scheduled sentencing date. The sentencing guidelines required 21 to 27 months of custodial time. My mouth was telling me I was ready for any decision, but my mind and body were getting nervous. Since Bishop Jakes already had command of the room, I asked him if he could pray for my posture as I headed down the stretch. Instantly, he, Pastor Battle and Pastor John Jenkins placed their hands on me, and he began to pray.

ACKNOWLEDGMENTS

Keith Battle helped me open this book. William Curtis helped me identify my loose hanging threads. Michael Walrond showed me the road to now. Tony Dungy gave me a daily spiritual diet. Jay-Z kept me confident. And Marvin Sapp filled my soul. Platforms, books and music helped me understand and process my exposure. Many prayed for me—some I was aware of and some I wasn't. Some called and or texted. Some wanted to do the same but didn't know how it would be received. I'm thankful to all who even thought about me and my family.

I'm thankful for the presence of Reverend Bob Gray, Pastor Jerry Birch, and all of the NBA Chaplains throughout the league. I appreciated the constant touch of Bishop John Borders III, Minister Glenn Wilson and Fred Crawford. To my "cousin brothers" Terry, Sam, I love y'all. To my favorite second cousins, lol, Corn and Shank, thanks for allowing me to be your little big cousin. To my circle of friends, Levan, Edward, Frank, Craig, Andrew and Vince, thanks for shielding me, not only throughout my life, but also through the exposure. To Pat, Juan and Chuck, thanks for planting the coaching bug. To Lee Stetson, Fran Dunphy, Steve Bilsky, Harriet Joseph and Scott Romeika—my failure in character can never remove the significance you have in my life. To my favorite Penn Parent Sean Jones, thanks for not allowing me to hide. Deborah Fries, thanks for peeling back the layers.

And to every young man I coached during my tenure at Penn, I pray that even in my failure, you can extract something to push you forward in life.

I want to thank Wyc Grousbeck, Steve Pagliuca, Dr. James Cash and the entire Banner Seventeen, LLC ownership group for their compassion and support. This extension of gratitude goes toward Rich Gotham, Danny Ainge and Michael Zarren as well.

Brad Stevens, while the world marvels at your coaching ability, most don't know the husband, father and man you truly are. I feel blessed to be led by you.

Warren, since the Long Beach Pro Summer League, you've been a constant force in my career.

Ron Sullivan, you saved my life. And I'm forever in debt to you.

Mom, Dad, Cre and Shay, y'all rode the storm with me. To my children, Jerome II, Taylor, Jordyn, and Roman, I love y'all, and I thank y'all for standing in the mud right next to me.

Aida, I would be issuing a large quantity of disrespect if I even attempted to use the phrase "thank you" to symbolize my gratitude towards you. No words in the English Dictionary can capture it. In your complete essence, you leave me speechless.

I dedicate the 64,686 words of this manuscript to Tyrone Lamont Allen.

Alize nightclub, Paris, 1998.

ABOUT THE AUTHOR

Jerome Allen is an NBA assistant coach for the Boston Celtics. He is a graduate of the Wharton School of Business at the University of Pennsylvania, where, prior to joining the Celtics staff, he served as the John. R. Rockwell Head Coach of Men's Basketball. Beginning in 1995 as the 2nd Round draft pick of the Minnesota Timberwolves, his professional basketball career spanned 14 years, in 4 different NBA cities and 6 different countries throughout Europe. Since 1999, he has worked to create sustainable social impacts for youth from communities that struggle with educational and economic access. Drawing upon 19 years of experience in educational consulting and his own life, Jerome Allen actively supports and inspires students to develop their gifts through education. Allen is the father of four children. He and his wife, Aida, have been married since 1998.